Heinz A. Richter

Modern Greek Myths

PELEUS

STUDIEN ZUR

GESCHICHTE GRIECHENLANDS UND ZYPERNS

HERAUSGEGEBEN VON HEINZ A. RICHTER

BAND 89

HARRASSOWITZ VERLAG WIESBADEN
IN KOMMISSION

VORMALS VERLAG FRANZ PHILIPP RUTZEN
WWW.RUTZEN-VERLAG.DE

Heinz A. Richter

Modern Greek Myths

2019

HARRASSOWITZ VERLAG • WIESBADEN
IN KOMMISSION

Bis Band 74
Peleus
Studien zur Archäologie und Geschichte Griechenlands und Zyperns
Herausgegeben von Reinhard Stupperich und Heinz A. Richter
Band 89

Umschlagvignetten:
Umschlagbild: Holger Müller "Antike Kriegskosten"
Gegenüber Titelblatt: Innenbild einer Schale des Peithinosmalers, Berlin, Pergamonmuseum (CVA Berlin 2, Taf. 61).

Bibliografische Information der Deutschen Nationalbibliothek
Die Deutsche Nationalbibliothek verzeichnet diese Publikation in der Deutschen Nationalbibliografie; detaillierte bibliografische Daten sind im Internet über http://dnb.d-nb.de abrufbar.

Bibliographic information published by the Deutsche Nationalbibliothek
The Deutsche Nationalbibliothek lists this publication in the Deutsche Nationalbibliografie; detailed bibliographic data are available in the internet at http://dnb.d-nb.de

Printed in Germany on fade resistant and archival quality paper (PH 7 neutral).
Gesamtherstellung: Beltz Bad Langensalza GmbH, Bad Langensalza

www.harrassowitz-verlag.de

ISBN 978-3-447-11165-2
ISSN 1868-1476

CONTENT

"Die Sage hüllt Griechenland in makellosen Purpur. Die Genealogie der Mythologie ist weniger verdächtig, als die der Historiker. Weil die Geschichte schließlich ihre Gestalt verliert, während der Mythos sich immer weiter gestaltet. Weil die Geschichte Wahrheit ist, die falsch wird, während der Mythos etwas Falsches ist, das Gestalt annimmt."

Jean Cocteau, "Vorwort" zu *Griechenland* (Wien, München, Basel: Kurt Desch, 1955), p. 8.

Mythos ist "ταύτα δέ ἐγένετο οὐδέποτε, ἔστι δέ ἀεί
"was niemals geschah und immer ist".

Nach; Salustios (Neoplatonist), *Περί θεών και κόσμου* (On the Gods and the Kosmos), c. 4 Satz 9

INTRODUCTION

Ancient Greece was full of myths most of which had a real historical kernel. Thus the myth of the Trojan War is based on a real armed conflict. Up to Herodotus myths in a way substitued for historiography. Historiography began with him and myths became a medium which gave answers to the ethical questions of life. The myth found its way into poetry. Virgil is a typical example in the Roman world. Typical examples of this kind are the Edda and the Song of the Nibelungs (Nibelungenlied) in Northern and Western Europe. At the same time the myth becomes a vehicle of the discussion of ethical questions e.g. Goethe's Antigone.

The historiography emancipated itself from this as the examples of Thucydides, Livius and Tacitus demonstrate. Medieval historiography sometimes borrowed from myths. But since early modern times serious not ideologically oriented Western European historiography kept its distance from myths, legends and tales. What truly counts are sober facts and matter-of-fact interpretations.

But in modern Greece this is different. Greece not only inherited clientelism from the Ottomans - a political culture totally different from that in Western Europe - but also a basically different way of looking at the past. The vision of the antiquity the Greeks took over from the European philhellenes of the 19th century was a vision which had little in common with reality. The 19th century Greek was the *Romios* who like Odysseus two thousand years earlier had mange to survive 400 years of Ottoman occupation. Now he was confronted with the *Ellin* who the philhellenes presented to him and who had much more in common with Achilles and nothing with the reality.

Therefore it was not astonishing that the Greeks began trying to glorify the present by myths. The first myth was that of the secret schools. In the Ottoman Empire it was allegedly prohibited to teach the Greek children their mother tongue there were the so called *gryfa s'choleia* (γρυφά σχολειά) in which priests taught the children Greek in hidden rooms in monasteries and churches. Such a "hidden"school is presented in a famous painting of Nikolaus Gysis, a member of the Munich School in the 19th century. This painting entered modern Greek history when it was printed on the backside of a 200 Drachme note (see next page). In reality such schools did not exist at all. They belong in the realm of modern myths.[1]

Another myth which has survived to this day is that King Constantine I was a Germanophile. This myth is based on French propaganda in World War I. Constantine was an experienced soldier who wanted that Greece remained neutral because he knew that no matter on which side Greece entered the war it would suffer. Venizelos on the other hand wanted Greece to enter the war on the side of the Etente, hoping thus to realize the megali idea.

Behind the back of the King he invited the Entente to land troops in Salonika and erected a counter government there. With French help he managed to oust King Constantine and lead Greece into the war. After he had taken over he published a white book which among other things contained the correspondence of Kaiser Wilhelm II and his sister Queen Sophia. On the basis of Russian diplomatic documents of the time I was able to prove that these letters were forgeries.[2] But as the white book was published by Venizelos in the eyes of many Greeks it is the historical truth. The myth replaces to the historical truth.

---

1 Alki Aggelou, *To kryfo scholeio, Chroniko enos mythou* (Athens: Estia, 1997).

2 Heinz A. Richter, *Griechenland 1915-1917 im Spiegel russischer Akten* (Ruhpolding: Rutzen, 2016); and *Idem*, *Der Krieg im Südosten*: Band 2: *Makedonien 1915-1918* (Ruhpolding: Rutzen, 2014).

In the sector of contemporary history many such cases could be shown. But in this study only myths and legends shall be described and analyzed which came into being in the context of WW II and are still virulent. One myth which shows the past in a friendly light, and strokes the Greek soul, is the six-weeks-myth which shows that Hitler lost the second world war because of the Greeks. The chapter on the famine in winter 1941 corrects the myth that only the Germans were guilty of it. The chapter dealing with Max Merten shows that he was not the greatest war criminal as the Greeks consider him. The analysis of the Dekemvriana (December events of 1944) pulls apart the Cold War myth that events in December 1944 were a Communist insurrection.

The two chapters dealing with the reparations and the so-called occupation loan (κατοχικό δάνειο) show how legends are used to derive financial advantages from them.

As in all other English editions of my books I needed a final control by a native speaker. In this case it was my old friend Rodney Freeborg Ph. D. living in the US. I want to thank him most cordially for his readiness to correct the text.

THE SIX-WEEKS-MYTH

Hitler lost world war II because the Greeks courageously fought for six weeks and these six weeks were missing in autumn in front of Moscow

The repercussions of the myth today
Both statements have been refuted for a long time and have been unmasked as projections of delusions, as a myth but this was done only by historiography outside Greece. Outside Greece the Greek myth of the missing-six-weeks is noted with a shake of the head. But in Greek historical comprehension the myth is an established truth. The teaching of history in Greek schools contributes to this, because many teachers are convinced that the myth is true or they do not know it better. The imparting of the myth to students is regrettable because it leads to a wrong assessment of their own history but is has no serious consequences. If the myth were taught at the universities of the country this would be precarious, because many of the graduates rise to leading positions. But it becomes really bad if the myth is taught as the truth to the alumni of the officers' schools.

If a graduate of the military school climbs up to higher ranks doubts of the truth of the myth or consideration of it as nonsense become dangerous. The possible consequences I encountered myself. During the researches for my book on the Operation *Merkur* in Crete I met the former C.-in-C., general Manousos Paragioudakis, who praised my work. He acknowledged the work on Greek history which I had done the past decades by giving me a medal of honour.

When the Greek edition of this book was presented in Irakleion in 2011 he did me the honour by participating in the presentation. But when the presenter said that I had proved in this book as well that neither the Operation *Marita* (occupation of mainland Greece) nor Operation *Mercury* (occupation of Crete) had had any impact on Operation *Barbarossa* (attack on the Soviet Union) Paragioudakis stood up outraged, protested and left the room accompanied by his company. Later it was stated that a majority of the listeners had also left which was denied by eyewitnesses who had been present.

A few days later I received a letter in which the general accused me of making Goebbels propaganda. I preferred not to answer to this letter. But when in 2014 the University of Crete honoured me with a honorary doctorate he demanded in the newspaper of Rethymnon that the University should refrain from this. When the University did not obey he saw to it that the festivity of bestowal was disturbed so much that it could not even begin. The title was bestowed on me the following day in a lecture hall of the University in a totally un-solemn way.

Now in all Cretan media an agitation against me began. It was obvious that I had become the scape goat of Merkel and Schäuble to whom they could show what they thought of the politics of Berlin.

In a parallel manner the General made the judiciary to attack me by legal means. Some quotes of my book taken out of context were used to indict me as a Nazi propagandist on the basis of a new law against deniers of the holocaust. This law had been disputed from the beginning: A great number of Greek historians had protested against it because it could be misused - something which happened in my case.

I won the trial with the help of two brilliant Athenian lawyers but then the faculty which had bestowed me with the honorary doctorate came under pressure to recant it. This affair dragged on in a nasty way during the following years but by the help of Athenian friends - among them my friend Nikos Dimou - it came to nothing.

The whole affair in Crete was a farce. The General could not cope with the fact that I had unmasked the myth in which he believed and which is a part of his self-deception. The de-mythologization process got into the maelstrom of the anti-German campaign caused by the financial crisis and I was stamped a Nazi. In view of these facts it appears reasonable to confront the myth with the historical truth and to report its evolutionary history. Maybe this will contribute that in Greece this myth will be recognized as such.

The genesis of the myth

In order to understand the origins of the myth it is necessary to take a look at the British policy in the winter 1940/41. Shortly after the beginning of WW II the British government had to realise that it did not have enough weapons and its own productions was not sufficient. Thereupon the US government under Roosevelt developed the so-called cash-and-carry-program. Thus Britain could buy weapons by paying in cash. This functioned quite well until the fall of 1940. But towards the end of 1940 Churchill had informed Roosevelt that rather soon Britain would not have any foreign exchange and thus the cash-and-carry-program would end.[1] Thereupon Roosevelt developed the lend-lease-program which would enable the British to lease weapons. But in contrast to the first this program needed a legal basis. This meant that the law needed a passage by the US Congress which was neutralistic at that time. The hot phase of the parliamentary debate was between February and March 1941. If another country which had been guaranteed by Britain in March 1939 would be overrun by Hitler without any British intervention the rejection of the law would have been secure.[2] Roosevelt informed Churchill accordingly. Since Greece was the most probable victim of Hitler Churchill decided to intervene there,[3] secretly hoping that the real intervention needed not to take place because Hitler would overrun Greece before. Thus the real theme was not genuine help for Greece but the impression of this help on the public opinion in the US.

In January the Greek dictator Metaxas had rejected the first British help offer because it was totally inadequate consisting out of two infantry divisions and a tank brigade.[4] But at the end of January Metaxas all of a sudden died. His death made a second trial offer possible. The new British foreign secretary, Anthony Eden, was ordered to impose this help on the Greeks. But also the new Greek Prime Minister, Alexandros Koryzis, a former banker, also recognized immediately that the help offered was still totally inadequate. Indeed the British made the same offer as in January because they had no other troops available in the region. However to make the offer attractive to the Greeks it was inflated by fake offers. Koryzis understood what was go-ing on and wanted to reject the British offer but King George II who did not want to loose British favour forced Koryzis to accept it.[5]

How untrustworthy the help offer was, was shown by another development: During his talks the Greek C.-in-C., General Alexandros Papagos, had told Eden that Macedonia and

1 Winston Churchill, *The Second World War*, IV, *The Commonwealth Alone* (London: Cassell, 1964), p. 221.

2 Hellmuth G. Dahms, *Roosevelt und der Krieg. Die Vorgeschichte von Pearl Harbour* (München: Oldenbourg, 1958), p. 62; Martin Gilbert, *Winston Churchill*, VI, *Finest Hour 1939-1941* (London: Heinemann, 1983), p. 985; Heinz Richter, *Griechenland im Zweiten Weltkrieg August 1939 - Juni 1941* (Bodenheim: Syndikat, 1997), p. 174ff.

3 Robert L. Sherwood (ed.), *The White House Papers of Harry L. Hopkins*, I, (London, 1948), p. 239f; David Dilks (ed.), The Diaries of Sir Alexander Cadogan O.M. 1938-1945 (London: Cassell, 1971), p. 356f.

4 Richter, *op. cit.*, p. 155ff.

5 On Eden's Mission Richter, *op. cit.*, pp. 217-243.

Thrace could not be held in case of a German attack and had to be evacuated if Yugoslavia did not enter the war. Eden promised to take this matter up during his talks in Belgrade. Papagos let the Greek troops remain in Macedonia and was waiting for Eden's reply which, however, never arrived.

When Eden arrived in Athens again he learned that the Greek troops had not been withdrawn from Macedonia. As a typical politician he immediately accused Papagos not having kept his promise to withdraw the troops. Papagos rejected this accusation but even after the end of the war this controversy continued in the memoirs of the two adversaries. It entered history as the Papagos-Eden-controversy.

In the wake of Eden's visit to Belgrade there was a coup against the government which was friendly towards the Axis. But a coordination of the war preparations of Yugoslavia and Greece did not take place. The abnormal length of the winter disrupted Churchill's timing. The Lend-Lease-Law passed Congress in early March. But as the Germans could attack only in early April the British help had to be transported to Greece, indeed. Therefore the very successful British offensive towards Tripolis had to be stopped and the first troops were sent to Greece. The British staff in the Near East knew that it would be impossible to stop the German advance with the few British troops and began to make plans for their evacuation even before the first troops were shipped to Greece. The loss of all war material was accepted.[1]

The German attack which began in early April was the last *Blitzkrieg* of the *Wehrmacht.* The British inspired *coup d'état* in Belgrade shortened the offensive against Greece because the Greek defence position in Macedonia could be bypassed over Yugoslav territory. Greece was occupied in three weeks.[2]

After the end of the British expedition to Greece which ended in a fiasco at the end of April which could only be compared with the Norwegian debacle a year earlier murmurs began in the British public. In order to silence the critics and probably also to avoid a development similar to the one after the Norwegian debacle which had led to the fall of the Chamberlain Government and to the Churchill Government, and to stabilize Eden's position on 6 may 1931 the Government via Eden demanded from the House of Commons: *"That this House approves the policy of His Majesty's Government in sending help to Greece and declares its confidence that our operations in the Middle East and in all other theatres of war will be pursued by the Government with utmost vigour."* During his speech Eden avoided any concrete statement and remained very vague: During the talks on 22 February he had informed the Greeks about the strength of the troops to be sent which was a straightforward lie. At the end he reduced the whole complex on a moral problem: "*In this war we are fighting, not for gains, but for causes; and Greece is the embodiment of those causes. I believe that had we not gone to her help, we could not have raised our heads again.*"[3]

Though critical voices were heard but nobody demanded the resignation of the Government as it had been the case one year before after the Norwegian debacle. At the end of the debate Churchill rose to speak. In his remarkable speech he said that the ensuing voting would have a signalling effect in foreign countries. This caused the overwhelming majority of the House to comply and vote for him. In this vote he was assisted by the new chief whip, James Stuart. 447 deputies voted yes, only 3 voted "no" and they had not been the critiques during the debate. The overwhelming voting victory ended any other debate of the sense of the expe-

1 Robin Higham, *Diary of a Disaster. British Aid to Greece 1940-1941* (Lexington: The University Press of Kentucky, 1986), p. 166.

2 On the German attack on Greece Richter, *op. cit*, pp. 330-438.

3 *House of Commons Debates,* Vol. 371, cols. 727, 733.

dition to Greece and prevented Eden's mistakes from coming to the fore. When Churchill left the room deputies cheered him. Churchill looked very satisfied.[1] On 7 May 1941 Churchill's secretary, John Colville, noted in his dairy: "The PM went early to bed, elated by his forensic success."[2]

Three day later the attention of the public and of the critics was attracted by a new topic: Hitler's deputy, Rudolf Heß, landed in Scotland which led to wild speculations. Later in May and June the setbacks in Northern Africa and in Crete followed; the Hood and the Bismarck were sunk; and in June the intervention in Syria. These were all spectacular events which overshadowed the fiasco in Greece and it almost fell in oblivion.

But Eden knew that sooner or later the question of his role would be put therefore he began to search for a suitable answer. Some months later he found an argument which would silence all critics: When the Wehrmacht's advance towards Moscow got stuck in the autumn rains and the beginning of winter Eden said in a speech on 23 October 1941 in Manchester: *"Greece's brave defence upset the time-table of Hitler's plans and delayed his prearranged attack on Russia for at least six most important weeks. What would those six weeks of campaigning weather be worth to Hitler now?"*[3] A few days later Eden's secretary, Richard Law, asked himself what Hitler would give if he could get back the 42 days of the Greek campaign.[4] Thus we can date the birth of the myth on 23 October 1941.

Eden's and Law's remarks were unofficial and noncommittal remarks as they are made in a lecture to an arbitrary audience. But they were lacking the consecration of a statement in the House of Commons. But this followed two months later.

During a debate in the House of Commons on 8 January 1942 a Member of Parliament accused Eden that the expedition to Greece had been a *political and sentimental decision* and therefore totally wrong. Eden reacted irascibly: *"It is arguable, and will probably be arguable for an extremely long time, whether that decision was right or wrong, but it certainly was not a political and sentimental decision, as my colleagues are well aware. It was taken with the full advice and concurrence of the Chief of Staff and the commanders concerned. Whatever else the decision was, it was not political and it was not sentimental."* A deputy asked a further question: Did Eden earnestly claim that he had advised Wavell to discontinue his successful advance in Libya to intervene in Greece? Eden tried to excuse himself by stating that the decision to intervene in Greece produced the coup in Yugoslavia. When contradictions were heard Eden felt provoked: *"Now I will go a stage further. The Yugoslav coup d'état also resulted in a Yugoslav-Russian rapprochement which was also of very great importance, and finally the resistance of Yugoslavia and Greece did delay by at least six weeks the breaking of the main attack upon Russia. That also, I may say, was of the very greatest importance, of which I assure you our Allies are very well aware."*[5]

On 10 January 1942 the *TIMES* followed up by using Eden's arguments and claimed that the Greeks by their resistance had delayed Hitler's attack on the Soviet Union.[6] It was obvious that Eden tried to justify the failed attack withe the assistance of the *TIMES* and arguments ex post. But with his statement in the House of Commons and the article in the *TIMES* the myth

---

1 Nigel Nicolson (ed.), *Harold Nicolson, Diaries and Letters, 1939-1945* (London, 1967), p. 164f.

2 Gilbert, *op. cit.*, p. 1.084.

3 American Council on Public Affairs, (ed.), *The Greek White Book: Diplomatic Documents Relating to Italy's Aggression Against Greece* (Washington, 1943), p. 14. This is a reprint edition of the Greek White Book with some amendements by Tsouderos. Quoted from here on as *Greek White Book.*

4 *Ibidem*, p. 14.

5 *House of Commons Debates*, Vol. 37, col. 169.

6 *Greek White Book*, p. 16.

had acquired anew quality. Now it was reality because it could be read in the HoC proceedings and in the *TIMES*.

After the war there were differing opinions about the effect of the Greek campaign on *Barbarossa*. Wavell's biographer, Collins, formulate his critique cautiously: *"There are other facets to this fascinating problem but they are mostly in the nature of wisdom after the event. Hitler's fatal delay in opening the offensive against Russia ... can probably be attributed to the hard fighting and heavy losses the German armies underwent in Greece; this delay has been assessed as low as two weeks and as high as six. Should history support the latter assertion then it may be claimed that British intervention in Greece saved Russia and so materially helped to win the war."*[1] The argument with the losses was not valid in view of the small numbers.

A rather acrimonious critique stems from General de Guingand who had been in Greece in 1941 together with Eden. *"I believe Eden when justifying our intervention in Greece to the House, stated that our action had delayed Germany's attack on Russia by several weeks. Whether this is true or not, I suggest such a method of justification is similar to a punter who, having bought by mistake the wrong ticket at the tote, finds that horse wins, and then goes about saying 'What a clever boy am I!'"*[2] The British military historian Lidell Hart expressed similar thoughts: *"Selbst wenn der griechische Feldzug die Invasion Rußlands verzögerte, würde diese Tatsache nicht die von der britischen Regierung getroffene Entscheidung rechtfertigen, denn damals hatte sie dieses Ziel nicht vor Augen."*[3]

These critical remarks caused Buckley in his 1951 official history of the expedition to Greece to put a question mark to the six-weeks-thesis.[4] Since then serious British authors do not use this argument any more to justify the expedition to Greece. In 1952 a scholarly investigation of *Historical Branch of the UK Cabinet Office* came to the conclusion that the German campaign in the Balkans did not have any influence on the beginning of *Barbarossa*.[5] Eden himself was clever enough not to mention his thesis any more in his memoirs. Less serious authors, however, returned often to this attractive thesis.[6] In general the six-weeks-thesis did not appear in British historiography dealing with the expedition to Greece. Anthony Beevor put it in a nutshell when he wrote in 1991: *"The notion that the battles of Greece and Crete delayed Barbarossa with fatal effects was nothing more than wishful consolation."*[7]

The myth in Greece

The Greek side had attentively registered each remark which praised the victories of the Greek army over the Italians and acknowledged the courageous defence against the Germans. Such remarks delighted the sinister life of a government in exile. Such remarks proved the high evaluation of the Greeks by the Allies. But towards the end of 1942 certain events caused a total change of the character and significance of Eden's statement.

On 10 December 1942 the then Foreign Secretary of the US, Cordell Hull, made a official statement about the resurrection of a free and independent Albania after the war.[8] One day

---

1 Robert J. Collins, *Lord Wavell (1883-1941). A Military Biography* (London Hodder & Stoughton, 1947), p. 463.
2 Francis De Guingand, *Operation Victory* (London: Hodder & Stoughton, 1947), p. 77.
3 Basil Henry Liddell Hart, *Die Strategie einer Diktatur. Aufstieg und Fall deutscher Generale* (Zürich: Amsstutz, Herdeg, 1949), p. 157.
4 Christopher Buckley, *Greece and Crete 1941* (London: HMSO, 1952), p. 140.
5 Gavin Long, *Greece, Crete and Syria* (Canberra: Australian War Memorial, 1953), p. 193.
6 Robert Crisp, *The Gods Were Neutral. A Story of the Greek Campaign 1941* (London: White Lion, 1975), p. 7f.
7 Antony Beevor, *Crete. The Battle and the Resistance* (London: Kohn Murray, 1991), p. 230.
8 Text in: *Department of State Bulletin* (12 December 1942), p. 998.

later Foreign Secretary Eden told the Greek Prime Minister Tsouderos that Britain also would make such a statement; the Greek demands of Northern Epirus were known but they should be discussed after the end of the war. Tsouderos, PM of the Government in exile and his vice premier, Kanellopoulos, protested - the first in a restrained way, the other violently. Eden was not impressed and stuck to his statement.[1]

Tsouderos recognized that a similar fate threatened as after WWI: The military performance of Greece would again not be honoured by the Allies. In order to do something against this the Greek Government started a publicity campaign in the US which should influence public opinion in favour of Greece. One of the first measures was the re-publication of the Greek White Book on the conflict with Italy in 1940.

In the preface Tsouderos published a whole collection of six-weeks-quotes. Besides Eden's statements and other protagonists rather peripheral statements were published even statements in the press of South American states.[2] The aim was to impress US public of Greek military achievements so much that it would align itself with Greece's ambitions.[3] But until the end of the war the six-weeks-thesis remained an argument in Greece's public relations campaign.

But in 1945 the character of this thesis changed again. After the tragic evens of December 1944 (Dekemvriana) and the beginning of the Cold War in 1945 the Greeks began to ask themselves whether all their efforts had been in vain but now the well known Athenian journalist of Cypriot descent, Achilefs Kyrou, wrote a book with the significant title Η Ελλας έδοσε την νικην (Greece gave the victory) which contained quite a number of such statements which culminated in the thesis[4] that Hitler lost the war because of the brave Greek resistance the decisive six weeks in front of Moscow had been missing. On the one side this thesis was a continuation of the PR campaign of the war time and on the other side it was balm for the injured Greek and was repeated one year later in a special study: Though one was again disesteemed by the Allies but one had the uplifting feeling that in reality Greece had delivered the decisive contribution which cost Hitler the victory even if the Allies did not recognize this.

In the ensuing years this thesis was repeated so often that it became self-supporting and was the indubitable truth in the end: In the special edition of Στρατιωτική Επιθεορισή (Military Review) on the occasion of the 50 years return of the Italian attack this thesis was found and a year later a historical study appeared on the same topic.[5] Additionally the thesis was constantly embroidered and enriched by further "details".[6] The six-weeks-thesis became an inherent part of the national myth.[7]

---

1 Heinz Richter, *Griechenland zwischen Revolution und Konterrevolution 1936-1946* (Frankfurt: Europäische Verlagsanstalt, 1973), p. 180f.

2 *Greek White Book*, pp. 12 - 16.

3 After the war this argumentation was taken over by Greek-American Organisations. The aims of these pressure groups contained demands for the Dodekanese and Northern Epirus/Southern Albania and "Enosis", I. e. the unification of Cyprus with Greece as well as "border correction" at the expense of Yugoslawia and Bulgaria. See vgl. Peter A. Zervakis, *Justice for Greece, Der Einfluß einer gräkoamerikanischen Interessengruppe auf die Außenpolitik der USA gegenüber Griechenland, 1945-47*, (Stuttgart: Steiner, 1994), p. 61; about the propagandistic instrumentalisation of the "six-weeks-thesis" see. *Ibidem.*, pp. 94, 108, 114, 130 f.

4 Achillefs A. Kyrou, *I Ellas Edose tin Nikin* (Athen: Aetos, 1945), pp. 224ff.six

5 "To Epos tou '40" *Stratiotiki Epitheorisi* (July-September 1990), p. 21; Angeliki Dima-Dimitriou, "Ellinoitalikos polemos (1940-1941) enas oreinos agonas" *Stratiotiki Epitheorisi* (September-October 1991), p. 24.

6 Allegedly there had been radio transmissions by the Soviets in Greek in which they thanked the Greeks that they had kept back the Wehrmacht for six weeks and thus saved th Soviet Union.

7 The Yugoslavs developed a similar myth. The Serbian rebels and their adherents impeded with their coup 27 March 1941 the German occupation of Moscow: Nora Beloff, *Tito's Flawed Legacy, Yugoslavia and the West,*

Myths seem to play an important role in the lives of the nations but in this case there is an additional special development: In Greece's historical consciousness the six months struggle against the Italians in Epirus and Albania, the so-called Albanian Epos which had become a myth also, melted together with the six-weeks-myth into an entity.

There cannot be the slightest doubt that Greece can be proud about the deeds of her army and her people. At that time, the Greeks were the only nation which fought against Fascism and successfully defended her freedom. Greece set the same bright example as the Finns had done a year before against imperialistic Stalinism of the Soviet Union. This was something unusual in the Europe of 1940-41; Greece proved that even small nations could resist Fascist aggression. The accomplishments were inflated mythologically and glorified as the epos of '40. This process can be retraced and is understandable.

But it is ominous to link this epos directly with the myth of the missing six-weeks- Here something factual is linked with fiction as we will see. If this linkage were confined to a little informed public one could overlook it. But it is worrying that a part of the public considers doubts on the six-weeks-myth as attacks on the Greek army and reacts with fierce backlashes of the type which I described in the begin of this chapter. However really problematical is the fact a part of Greek scholarly research in Greece and abroad has taken over this thesis and propagates it as the historical truth.

In the early 1980s Andrew Zapantis devoted about 100 pages in his book on Greek-Russian relations between 1917 and 1941 to this question.[1] Zapantis' excursion is the biggest collection of quotes on this subject. But Zapantis' fervour to collect as many quotes as possible caused him to quote totally peripheral literature but he forgot important primary sources e.g. the war diary of the High Command of the Wehrmacht. Remarks by the US Chief of Staff George C. Marshall or the C.-in-C. of the Polish exile forces General Wladyslaw Anders sound interesting but do not contribute substantially the answer of this question.[2] Zapantis even consulted English translations of Soviet and East German literature which express apodictionally the same thesis.[3]

Additionally Zapantis especially analysed the meteorological conditions. Though his study contains some interesting details it is regrettable that Zapantis again arrived at the old conclusions when he quoted the in 1976 acting director of the historical department of the Greek General Staff, General Ioannis Palaiologos: *"It has been historically proven that it [the war of the Axis against Greece and the strong resistance of the Armed Forces of the latter] influenced considerably the entire course of World War II and particularly it delayed the date of the German invasion of Russia ... Thus, the attack against Russia could have started perhaps as of May 15, in which case there would have been adequate time for the occupation of Moscow, or for the manifestation of a more decisive perhaps action toward the Caucasus."*[4] The weight of Palaiologos statement rests only on the authority of his position. He never stood out as an intimate connoisseur of historical literature. Moreover he did not know German which limited his knowledge considerably.

The six-weeks-myth in Germany

1939-84, (London: Victor Gollancz, 1985), p. 65.

1 Andrew l. Zapantis, *Greek-Soviet Relations, 1917-1941* (New York: Columbia University Press, 1982) = East European Monographs, No. CXI, Boulder, pp. 498 - 593.

2 *Ibidem*, p. 514.

3 *Ibidem*, p. 498ff.

4 *Ibidem*, p. 592.

The myth was not only influential in Greece but astoundingly also in Germany. The first person who claimed that the Greek or Balkan campaign had cost the operation Babarossa the decisive six weeks was Hitler himself. On 15 February 1945 he complained in his air-raid shelter underneath the Reich's Chancellery that the idiotic Italian attack on Greece had hindered him to begin the attack on the Soviet Union a few weeks earlier. Two days later he repeated this statement and added that the senseless Italian attack on Greece and the ignominious defeats there led to te changeover of the Yugoslavs and forced him to intervene in the Balkans. Thus he lost some of his best divisions. Without the Italian participation in the war he could have started the war on 15 May.[1]

These statements were a transparent justification attempt: Hitler knew that the war was lost and was searching for excuses for his failure which would leave the Führer legend unhurt after the final catastrophe. Hitler's arguments are monocausal attempts to explain complex events which led to his failure.[2]

During the Nuremberg trial air force chief Göring made similar statements. He alleged that the necessity to intervene in the Balkans caused a postponement of the attack on Russia from 15 May to the second half of July.[3] The other two co-defendants, the chief of the Wehrmacht high command, Wilhelm Keitel, and the chief of the Wehrmacht's staff, Alfred Jodl, were more restrained in their statements. Keitel stressed that Mussolini's attack had taken place without Hitler's knowledge. The Italian difficulties in Albania had causes German intervention. When on 27 March 1941 the attack on Yugoslavia had been discussed he and Jodl had turned against a postponement of the attack on the Soviet Union.[4] Zapantis could not locate any argument of Keitel and Jodl that the attack on the Soviet Union had been postponed because of the Balkan campaign. However the Quartermaster I of the army, general Friedrich Paulus who had been involved in the planning of the campaign against Russia alleged during interrogation that by the attack on Yugoslavia the begin of *Barbarossa* had been postponed by five weeks.[5]

The explanation for Göring's statement is rather simple. He was seeking a suitable protecting argument to cover the defeat which on the one hand would not damage the image of Hitler and of the regime and on the other hand avoided the admission that the campaign against Russia had been lost because of their own mistakes. Operation *Barbarossa* had been lost because of lack of time; this was a face saving excuse. Göring could not admit that Hitler had played va banque and had lost. The behaviour of Keitel and Jodl during the interrogations confirms this assumption. As they were not ready to tell straightforward lies they preferred to keep their statements vague. Paulus' statement which at a first glance looks credible emerges as rathe weak. Paulus had not participated at the decisive session on 26 March 1941. His testimony rested on hear-say. Additionally he preferred the six-weeks-thesis because it deviated from the fact that the *Barbarossa* campaign which he had planned had failed.

Andrew Zapantis took trouble to collect all pertinent statements out of the memoirs of German Generals and Admirals published in the 1950s and 1960s. Thee was not one higher

---

1 Adolf Hitler, *Le Testament Politique de Hitler. Notes recueillies par Martin Bormann* (Paris: Fayard, 1959), pp. 95, 105, 107.

2 Andreas Hillgruber, *Hitlers Strategie. Politik und Kriegführung 1940 - 1941* (Frankfurt: Bernard & Graefe, 1965), p. 506.

3 Zapantis, *op. cit.*, p. 504.

4 *Ibidem*, p. 506.

5 Internationaler Militärgerichtshof, *Der Prozeß gegen die Hauptkriegsverbrecher vor dem Internationalen Militärgerichtshof Nürnberg* (Nürnberg, 1947), VII, p. 286. *"Infolge seines Entschlusses, Jugoslawien anzugreifen, mußte der voraussichtliche Termin für den Angriffsbeginn um etwa fünf Wochen verschoben werden, das heißt auf die zweite Junihälfte."*

officer who did not use the six-weeks-argument as an excuse for the defeat. The former navy chief Erich Raeder wrote that the campaigns against Yugoslavia and Greece delayed the attack on Russia. In April Hitler allegedly ordered that end all measures which might be interpreted as preparations for an attacked should be postponed. General Walter Warlimont who had been chief of the defence was of the same opinion. He wrote that the attack on the Soviet Union had to be postponed from the middle of May to the 22 July and the deployment plan had to be worked over.[2]

The then chief of staff of the C.-in-C. West, and later chief of the 4th Army, general Günther Blumentritt alleged even that the planing of operation *Barbarossa* had been interrupted by the Balkan campaigns. But he adds that *Barbarossa* could not have begun on 15 May because one would been force to wait until the fields had dried after the snowmelt. The Balkan campaign had retarded the begin of *Barbarossa* by 5½ weeks but because thawing began late in 1941 *Barbarossa* could not have begun earlier.[3]

The (civilian) diarist of the war diary of the Wehrmacht, Helmuth Greiner, stated in his memoirs that the Balkan campaign retarded the begin of operation *Barbarossa* but he avoided making this clearer. His statement is interesting that the withdrawal of the VIII air force corps employed in Crete created difficulties.[4] The C.-in-C. of Army Group South, field marshal Gerd von Rundstedt reported that the preparations of his army group had been impeded by the late arrival of the tanks divisions which had been deployed in the Balkans. His leader of the tank units, general Ewald von Kleist, however admitted that the number of troops deployed in the Balkans had been small in comparison with those deployed against the Soviet Union but the number of the tank units had been high and the tanks had to be restored. But Army Group South played a minor role in the operation *Barbarossa*; decisive was the Army group in the middle and this did not lack any tanks.[5]

General Kurt v. Tippelskirch who as quartermaster IV in the general staff of the army was responsible for tactical reconnaissance wrote in his history of WWII: *"Eine wesentliche Änderung des ursprünglich vorgesehenen Zeitablaufs brachte der jugoslawische Feldzug mit sich. Zugleich mit dem Befehl für den Aufmarsch gegen Jugoslawien mußte die Verschiebung des Beginns von 'Barbarossa' um mindestens vier Wochen befohlen werden. Für den Rußlandfeldzug gingen fünf unbezahlbare Wochen verloren, die wohl nicht ohne entscheidenden Einfluß auf sein Ergebnis geblieben sind."*[6] Admiral Kurt Assmann, who was the highest historian of the navy wrote that the Yugoslav campaign retarded *Barbarossa* by five weeks.[7]

The chief of the general staff of the army, Halder, who knew the true facts better than anyone else wrote in a letter to the British General Alexander that he Balkan campaign did not delay the attack on the Soviet Union. Operation *Marita* had some influence on operation *Barbarossa* but it did not disturb the deployment of the troops for *Barbarossa*. The rapid collapse of the Yugoslavia and the front in Northern Greece enabled an early return transport so that these troops were availably for the deployment against Russia. The few troops which advanced to the southern Peloponnese could be brought back in time so that they were available as reserves for *Barbarossa*. Additionally the attack on Russia could not begun

---

1 Erich Raeder, *Mein Leben* (Tübingen: Schlichtenmayer, 1957), II, p. 250.
2 Walter Warlimont, *Im Hauptquartier der Wehrmacht* (Frankfurt: Athenäum, 1964), p. 145.
3 Zapantis, *op. cit.*, p. 509.
4 *Ibidem*, p. 511.
5 Liddell Hart, *op. cit.*, p. 157.
6 Kurth v. Tippelskirch, *Geschichte des Zweiten Weltkriegs* (Bonn: Athenäum, 1959), p. 175.
7 Kurt Assmann, *Deutsche Schicksalsjahre. Historische Bilder aus dem Zweiten Weltkrieg und seiner Vorgeschichte* (Wiesbaden: Brockhaus, 1950), p. 222.

earlier than July because of the spring inundation. And at that time the units deployed in the Balkans had returned long before.[1] Halder's statements should be taken with some reserve because he had different opinions here and then.

Also some well known German military historians propagate the six-weeks-thesis. In his history of the German general staff Walter Görlitz expressed the opinion that the Serbian-Greek campaign delayed the operation *Barbarossa* by one month. Even in the reknowned works of Jacobson and Rohwer one finds this thesis.[2] Therefore it is not astonishing that even in 1994 in a popular science work the six-weeks-thesis was presented as the truth.[3]

It is striking that of German publications which emphasized the six-weeks-thesis in an outspoken way, that their authors had been far away from the decision centres in 1941. All their statements are based on hear-say. No court would ever accept their testimony. In view of the importance of this question it seems reasonable to have second look at the relevant sources.

The myth and historical facts

Hitler's order no. 20 for operation *Marita* (the attack on Greece) was signed on 13 December 1940, the order no. 21 for operation *Barbarossa* on 18 December 1940. Both order were the final points of developments which had begun earlier. The necessary decisions had been taken earlier: the one for the attack on Greece in early November and that on the attack on the Soviet Union at the end of November. The planning of the basic feature had begun even six months earlier namely towards the end of July 1940.

On 5 December 1940 at 3 p.m. the C.-in-C. of the Wehrmacht v. Brauchitsch, the chief of the general staff of the army Halder, the chief of the high command of the Wehrmacht, Keitel, and the chief of the staff of the Wehrmacht Jodl met with Hitler in the Reichs Chancellery. The main weight of the discussion wee the operations *Marita* and *Barbarossa* . Brauchitsch presented the plan for *Marita* and linked it with *Barbarossa* : *Marita* might begin the earliest after snow melting in the middle of March. Presumably the operation would last until the middle of April. The retransport of the troops would need four weeks and their refreshment some time also. *"Obwohl diese Kräfte für die Ostoperation nicht zu entbehren seien, müsse diese möglichst frühzeitig beginnen, um die für die Operationen günstige Jahreszeit voll ausnützen zu können."*[4] For the C.-in-C. of the Wehrmacht it was clear from the beginning that the troops of *Marita* would be missing at *Barbarossa* but he did not see any reason why the campaign against should be postponed.

After this Hitler spoke. In order to exclude a British attack on German sphere of interest the attack an Greece had to be prepared. Should this be unnecessary because the Greeks finished the war with Italy nevertheless the deployment would be useful because these forces could be used against Russia. Then Hitler spoke about the timing. The attack against Greece would begin in early March and would end at the end of March or even at the end of April depending on the situation. In the latter case not all troops would be needed to the very end. Yugoslavia would join Germany when the Albanian front was stabilized. Closing the meeting

1 Alexander of Tunis, *The Alexander Memoirs* (London, 1962), p. 144f.

2 Walter Görlitz, *Der deutsche Generalstab. Geschichte und Gestalt 1667 - 1945* (Frankfurt: Verlag der Frankfurter Hefte, 1950?), p. 558. Rudolf Hofmann, "Die Schlacht von Moskau 1941", in: Hans-Adolf Jacobsen, Jürgen Rohwer, (eds.), *Entscheidungsschlachten des zweiten Weltkrieges* (Frankfurt: Bernard & Graefe, 1960), p. 139.

3 Jochen Brennecke, et al, *Der Zweite Weltkrieg: Balkan und Afrika* (Rastatt: Moewig, 1994), pp. 25, 30. This account is very tendentious and full of mistakes.

4 Hans-Adolf Jacobsen, (ed.), *Kriegstagebuch des Oberkommandos der Wehrmacht*, I, (Frankfurt: Bernard & Graefe, 1965), p. 203f. Quoted as *KTB OKW*.

Hitler ordered, *"die Vorbereitungen für das Unternehmen Marita und den Ostfeldzug in vollem Umfang zu treffen ... Der Ostfeldzug würde frühestens Mitte Mai beginnen, falls der Winter normal verlaufe."*[1]

Thus on 5 December 1940 the most important elements had been decided. The operations *Marita* and *Barbarossa* would be linked and had to be coordinated. The attack on Greece would take place in March/April. The time limits (minimal four, maximal eight weeks) for this operation were generously dimensioned and were undercut be far as became visible when the operation was realized. As it was noted in the war diary of the Wehrmacht on 6 December *Barbarossa* would begin the earliest in the middle of May.[2] In order no. 20 of 13 December the details were taken down and the link to operation *Barbarossa* established.

Thus the Führer's order no. 21 read: *"Die deutsche Wehrmacht muß drauf vorbereitet sein, auch vor der Beendigung des Krieges gegen England Sowjetrußland in einem schnellen Feldzug niederzuwerfen ... Den Aufmarsch ... werde ich gegebenenfalls acht Wochen vor dem beabsichtigten Operationsbeginn befehlen. Vorbereitungen, die eine längere Anlaufzeit benötigen, sind - soweit noch nicht geschehen - schon jetzt in Angriff zu nehmen und bis zum 15. 5. 41 abzuschließen ... Die beabsichtigten Vorbereitungen aller Wehrmachtsteile sind mir, auch in ihrem zeitlichen Ablauf, über das Oberkommando der Wehrmacht zu melden."*[3]

This of course did not mean that the attack on the Soviet Union would begin on 15May 1941 as it is often wrongly claimed.[4] The Führer order no. 21 determined only the date when th preparations of the operation *Barbarossa* should be completed. The order for the actual attack would be given later. *"15 May, therefore, was nothing but a provisional terminus post quem, and explicitly defined as such."*[5] Indeed it was snot yet clear whether Hitler really wanted to attack the Soviet Union. Brauchitsch at least considered it possible that Hitler was bluffing, and Hitler himself constantly stressed that he reserved all rights to take decisions: on 9 January 1941 Hitler removed any existing doubts: Operation *Barbarossa* would take place.[6] During the following weeks the High Command of the Army (OKH) worked out the orders for the deployment which Hitler approved on 31 January 1941.

The principles of the plan were rather simple The deployment would take place over a lengthy period rather slowly and only towards the end would the transports be increased. Thus the deployment could be done in disguise and the economic strain by the blockade of the railways could be kept at a minimum. In the final stage the "fast" units would be moved forward, i.e. the Panzer and motorized units. The deployment would take place in four phases. The first echelon was being moved east at the time when the deployment plan was submitted. By mid-March the transports of the second echelon into the rearward areas would begin and end by mid-April. In early April negotiations with Hungary should begin about the transport of the third echelon. For its transport almost the whole railway net of Hungary would be necessary. From then onward the deployment could no longer be tarnished. But the movement of the "fast" units their deployment in April and May would become obvious. There would be difficulties when the eight divisions of operation *Marita* would be retransported. In a fifth phase a strategic reserve force was to be built up. Hitler was satisfied with the plan and said

1 *Ibidem*, p. 204f.
2 *Ibidem*, p. 211.
3 Walther Hubatsch, (ed.), *Hitlers Weisungen für die Kriegführung 1939 - 1945* (München: DTV, 1965), p. 96f.
4 Hillgruber, *op. cit.*, p. 369 footnote 90.
5 Martin van Creveld, "The German Attack on the USSR: the Destruction of a Legend" *European Studies Review* 2:1 (1972), p. 71.
6 *KTB OKW*, I, p. 269.

that the whole world would hold its breath when the operation *Barbarossa* began.[1] Later some details were changed but the original great concept was not changed.

In contrast to this the deployment against Greece created troubles. Originally a tank group had been designated for the attack. But on 11 December 1940 the 12th Army was assigned for this operation. The High Command of the army (OKH) elaborated a deployment plan which provided for operation *Marita* that the troops were to be deployed in three echelons in Rumania until 25 January 1941 and in such a way that they could enter Bulgaria within twelve hours and cross the Greek border in 35 days.[2] However, the necessity to build bridges over the Danube and to fortify the existing ones compelled a postponement of the date for the attack on 6 March. Rumanian objections against the total take over of the railways led to a postponement. Massive snow storms in December and thawing in January and renewed snowfall slowed down the deployment and the building of the bridges. In the beginning of January the original deployment plan had been already retarded by two weeks.[3]

In the meantime the German efforts to make the Yugoslavs permit that the Germans could use their railways failed. In the end, the delay was six weeks and it was decided to cross the Danube on 1 March. On the 25 March finally the deployment of the 12th Army was finished and the attack could begin on 1 April. If the occupation of Greece succeeded in the time span provided for it *Barbarossa* could begin punctually.

But on 27 March 1941 the coup took place in Belgrade. As this might cause a threat from the flank of operation *Barbarossa* Hitler ordered the attack on Yugoslavia at a meeting of the military leadership. During this meeting an ominous sentence was uttered: *"In diesem Zusammenhang muß der Beginn der Barbarossa-Unternehmung bis zu 4 Wochen verschoben werden."*[4] At a first glance this sentence seems to be an order to postpone operation *Barbarossa*. But if one takes a closer look one discovers that the sentence contains an assumption. It is stated that the Yugoslav operation might lead to a postponement of *Barbarossa*. The wording "*bis zu 4 Wochen*" (up to four weeks) confirms this; an order would have sounded thus *"wird der Beginn ... um vier Wochen verschoben.*" (The start will be postponed by four weeks). An order with such an imprecise expression of time would have been impossible.

Had this sentence been an order it would certainly have found its way into the war diary of the OKW (High Command of the Wehrmacht) but there one does not find any order in this sense. But this sentence has become the basis of all later assertions that the Balkan campaign caused a postponement of the beginning of *Barbarossa*.

Moreover it is not known who said this sentence. If Hitler had said it thee is no doubt that it would have found its way into the protocol. It is possible that this warning was said by one of the officers present, a warning about which Halder spoke in his letter to the British general Alexander: *"The German General Staff therefore advised Hitler that the advance against Russia planned for mid-May might have to be postponed for six weeks. This deliberately overcautious estimate was not borne out by events."*[5] However this may be, this sentence is a statement or assumption but in no case an instruction or order for a postponement as is broadly believed. The only earwitnesses who heard this sentence and spoke about it later were Göring,

1 *KTB OKW*, I, p. 299f; Martin L. Van Creveld, *Hitler's Strategy 1940 - 1941. The Balkan Clue* (Cambridge: Cambridge University Press, 1973), p. 150.

2 *KTB OKW*, I, p. 224.

3 *Ibidem*, p. 114.

4 *ADAP*, XII, 1, p. 308; in the popular scientific account published by Moewig-Verlag the text was altered. Brennecke, *op. cit.*, p. 29.

5 Alexander, *op. cit.*, p. 144.

Keitel, Jodl and Halder.[1] All other authors write on hearsay. The question is whether this was done on purpose or not? The answer must remain open.

All the authors who insist that Hitler gave an order on 27 March to postpone operation Barbarous overlook a very simple fact: Hitler needed not give an order to postpone operation *Barbarous* because there did not yet exist an order on the beginning of *Barbarous* .[2] A volition by Hitler had certainly found its way in the OKW war diary. As Creveld has proved the OKW was of the opinion that *Barbarossa* would begin around 1 June.[3] The only result of the meeting on 27 March was Hitler's order no. 25 the order to attack Yugoslavia which was to coordinated with the attack on Greece. On 29 March it was decided that both attacks were to begin on the same day. One day later Hitler spoke to the commanders of army groups and army commanders. Afterwards there was a detailed discussion of operation *Barbarossa* .[4] No orders were given which would certainly have found their way into the war dairy of the OKW. On 6 April the attack on Yugoslavia and Greece began.

The impacts of operations 25, Marita and Merkur

Which influence did the attack on Yugoslavia have on operation *Marita* and *Barbarossa* ? Did the campaign in the Balkans cause a postponement? The actual fighting of the Yugoslav campaign lasted a bit more than a week; formally the campaign ended operation 25, the Yugoslav campaign, on 18 April 1941 when Yugoslavia surrendered. The Yugoslav campaign was one of Hitler's shortest Blitzkriegs. Operation *Marita* also began on 6 April 1941and ended as far the Greeks were concerned on 20 April with their surrender. The last British units left Greece on 28 April. After that there was a pause until 20 May when the attack on Crete began. Operation *Merkur* ended on 31 May.

Thus the real fighting lasted in Greece, i.e *Marita* a little over 2 weeks and *Merkur* a little less than 2 weeks, altogether 4 weeks. But really the Greeks fought only 3 days until the surrender in Macedonia. Then the withdrawal from Albania began. If one adds the four weeks negotiation pause to it the sum is eight weeks. But in Greece one did not check the addition and adopted Eden's six weeks.

Even if a postponement order had been given during the Yugoslav campaign the shortness of the campaign would have made it possible to repeal it. But this was not necessary because no such order had been given.

The second often heard assumption that the Yugoslav campaign had dislocated the deployment for *Barbarous* and retarded the attack on the Soviet Union is also not tenable. The attack on Yugoslavia came from two directions, from the North (Graz) and the East (Sofia). The deployment in the East did not have any effect, because the 12th Army was already there, with its seven corps and its 18 divisions and reinforced regiments as well as a

---

1 The following persons participated in the meeting: Hitler, Luftwaffenchef Herrmann Göring, OKW-Chef Wilhelm Keitel, der Chef des Wehrmachtführungsstabs Alfred Jodl, der Oberbefehlshaber des Heeres Walther v. Brauchitsch, der Generalstabschef des Heeres Franz Halder, Außenminister Joachim v. Ribbentrop, dessen Vertreter in Hitlers Hauptquartier Walter Hewel, der deutsche Militärattaché in Rom, Enno v. Rintelen, der zufällig in Berlin war, Luftwaffengeneral Karl Heinrich Bodenschatz, Hitlers Adjutant Oberst Rudolf Schmundt, Hitlers Marineadjutant Fregattenkapitän Karl-Jesco v. Puttkammer, Oberstleutnant Scherff vom OKW, Major v. Below, Major Christian, der Chef der Operationsabteilung des Generalstabs des Heeres, Oberst Adolf Heusinger, der Adjutant des Oberbefehlshaber des Heeres, Oberstleutnant Sievert, Luftwaffengeneral Hoffmann v. Waldau und Oberst Schmidt.

2 Also in Long, *op. cit.*, p. 193 on the Basis of a detailed monograph, which hat been compiled in March 1952 by the *Enemy Documents Section of the Historical Branch of the UK Cabinet Office*.

3 Creveld, *Hitler's Strategy*, p. 151.

4 *Ibidem*, p. 373.

tank group and had only to be redirected.[1] The units of the 2nd Army which was to attack from Graz had to transported there. But Creveld proved[2] only four divisions had to be withdrawn from the huge contingent provided for *Barbarous* . It did not disturb the deployment against the Soviet Union because those troops belonged to the second wave and had not yet been moved east. When they were sent South towards Yugoslavia other units of the reserve were moved east. Not a single one division sent to Yugoslavia belonged to the third echelon of the deployment against Russia. A few belonged to the fourth echelon but most of them were transferred from France whee they had been waiting for other operation after operation Felix (conquest of Gibraltar) had been cancelled. *"The delay caused by the outbreak of the Yugoslav campaign to the build-up for 'Barbarous' was limited to the time needed to prepare the OKH reserves for transportation. Even this delay, however, could be made up later on because of the very leisurely timetable governing stage III."*[3]

In other words: The deployment of *Barbarous* was not disturbed at all by the deployment against Yugoslavia. The often heard opinion that the campaign against Yugoslavia led to a postponement is absurd; it lasted scarcely a week. One could turn it around 180 degrees as John Lukacs did it: *"Hitlers schließliche Niederlage im Osten ist merkwürdigerweise vielleicht nicht auf den jugoslawischen Widerstand, sondern eher auf den überraschend schnellen Zusammenbruch der jugoslawischen und griechischen Streitkräfte zurückzuführen, durch die Hitler allzu selbstsicher wurde. Hätten seine Soldaten auf dem Balkan zwei Monate lang zu kämpfen gehabt, hätte er den Ostfeldzug um einen weiteren Monat, vielleicht sogar auf 1942 verschieben müssen."*[4]

The synchronous attack on Yugoslavia meant for *Marita* a real relief and saving of time. Now the fortified Metaxas line could bypassed via Yugoslavia and the Alikamon line could be outflanked which shortened the campaign against Greece enormously. One might even say that the British inspired coup in Belgrade made the attack an Greece much easier. Additionally the German military could use the Yugoslav railways. Thus the re-transport of the troops employed in Greece was much easier and quicker. Pointedly one could state that Yugoslav campaign made the Greek campaign easier and shortened it considerably.

But what about the campaign in Greece? Did it lead to a delay? The answer is again no. Creveld proved convincingly that operation *Marita* did not have any influence on the beginning of operation *Barbarous* .[5] The adherents of the six-weeks-myth assume that operation *Marita* absorbed great masses of troops until the very end. Well, it is correct that the German general staff had totally overestimated the forces in Greece and had made the 12th Army very strong. It consisted of seven army corps and a tank group, altogether 21 divisions among them five tank divisions and three mountain divisions.[6] But only a small fraction was used against Greece. Macedonia and Western Thrace was occupied by the 18th and 30th Mountain corps. The Vermion and Aliakmon positions were occupied by the same units but

1 A compilation of the units of the 12th Army on 5 April 1941 is found in *KTB OKW*, I, p. 134.

2 *Ibidem*.

3 *Ibidem*, p. 153.

4 John Lukacs, *Der letzte europäische Krieg 1939-1941* (München: DTV, 1980), p. 115.

5 Creveld, *Hitler's Strategy*, p. 172ff.

6 The 16th tank division was directly under the 12th Army. *Panzergruppe* 1 hat the 4th mountain division and the 294 the infantry under its command. The various army corps consisted out of these units: XVIII. Gebirgskorps (5. und 6. Gebirgs-, 72. Infanteriedivision, reenforced Infanterie-Regiment 125, 2. Panzerdivision), XXX. Korps (50., 164. Infanteriedivision), XXXX. motorisiertes Korps (9. Panzerdivision, SS-Regiment "AH", 73. Infanterieivision), XIV. motorisiertes Korps (5. Panzer-, 11. Panzer-, 60. mot. Division), XXXXI. motorisiertes Korps (SS "Reich", Infanterieregiment Großdeutschland), XL. Korps (76., 198. Infanteriedivision), L. Korps (46. Infanteriedivision). *KTB OKW*, I, p. 1.134.

some of its subordinated units had already been withdrawn. After the surrender of the Greek army only four units advanced further south: The SS-Divisions LAH (Leibstandarte Adolf Hitler) west of the Pindus, and the 5th and 6th Mountain divisions and the 5th tank division. Already on 29 April the re-transports of the troops began in central and southern Greece. On 14 May only three tank divisions and 15 infantry divisions were still in the Balkans. At the end of May the 5th tank division and SS division had left Greece. Thus not one unit which was deployed for *Barbarossa* remained there.

On 21 June only six divisions were still in the Balkans, while 117 infantry divisions, 17 tanks and 15 mobile divisions were deployed for *Barbarossa* , all together 195 divisions.[1] The idea that this enormous force would have to wait for the few units deployed against Greece is absurd.

There is however a fact which seems to contradict this and creates the impression that the Balkan operations had an impact on the planning of *Barbarous* : On 4 April new deployment plans were drawn which provided mid-June for the begin of the attack. At a first glance this seems to be the four weeks which were talked about. The third phase of the deployment should begin one week earlier i.e. on 8 April but they wee to be extended far longer until 20 May. Instead of the original railway schedule which was to reach a maximum from mid-April it was extended so much that the civil rail traffic was not disturbed until the end of May. The fourth phase was divided in two: between 23 May and 2 June infantry divisions would transported. During the last phase the maximal transport capacity of the railway should used to transport the "fast" units, i.e. the 12 tank and 12 motorized divisions to their advanced positions.[2]

But when on 12 April it became clear that the Yugoslav campaign would soon be over and in Greece the end also became visible because the British troops withdrew the High Command of the Army (OKH) stopped sending further troops to the 2nd and 12th army. Thus the latest opportunity after the surrender of Yugoslavia that the deployment of troops against Russia could have been accelerated again if it had been slowed down because of operation 25 (Yugoslavia).[3] But this did not happen. Instead on 22 April the operation group of the staff of the Wehrmacht recognized that the transports would be concluded on 23 June and stated that the begin of operation *Barbarous* had been fixed on 23 June. But was not yet the final decision yet. Finland was to be informed on 25 May and not as so far planned on 15 May.[4] Creveld proved that the troops returning from the Balkans had enough time for recreation and refreshment. - he speaks of 10 to 20 days - until they were moved east.[5]

Thus the question remains whether operation *Merkur*, the occupation of Crete, had any influence on the beginning of *Barbarossa* . The answer was negative also: Operation *Merkur* was executed by two Air Force units, the VIII and XI flying corps. The XI corps consisted of parachutists and air borne troops. It suffered terrible losses: 5,000 dead, missing and wounded. Of the 500 transport planes 150 wee destroyed and 165 damaged.[6]

---

1 *KTB OKW*, I, Anhang; Boris Semjonowitsch Telpuchowski, *Die sowjetische Geschichte des Großen Vaterländischen Krieges 1941-1945* (Frankfurt: Bernard & Graefe, 1961), p 35 footnote 1.

2 *Ibidem*, p. 171.

3 Vgl. die etwas verquere Logik bei J. R. M. Butler, *Grand Strategy*, II, *September 1939 - June 1941* (London: HMSO, 1957), p. 541.

4 KTB OKW, I, 384.

5 Creveld, *op. cit.*, p. 173.

6 Detlev Vogel, "Das Eingreifen Deutschlands auf dem Balkan", in: Militärgeschichtliches Forschungsamt (ed.), *Das Deutsche Reich und der Zweite Weltkrieg*, III, *Der Mittelmeerraum und Südosteuropa* (Stuttgart: Deutsche Verlagsanstalt, 1984), p. 509.

The heavy losses of the parachutists made Hitler forbid similar operations thus Cyprus was spared a similar fate as Crete. But operation *Merkur* had no impact on *Barbarossa* because already in Führer order no. 18 Hitler had ordered that parachutists during the first phase of the attack would be used only against punctual tactical target like such as railway or road bridges. The losses of the VIII Flying Corps were felt during this phase but could be replaced soon. The losses did no have any impact on *Barbarossa* .[1]

Right from the beginning of the planning of *Barbarossa* it had been clear that the Luftwaffe (air force) would play a subordinate role. All orders show that the Luftwaffe would have tactical tasks supporting the attacks of the infantry and tanks. It would not take over strategical tasks as it did not have any long range bombers which might have bombarded the industrial centres beyond the Ural.[2] Operation *Merkur* hit the transport fleet heavily but the fighting units had small losses[3] compared with those it suffered during the battle of Britain and from which it never recovered. These losses and the dispersal on many fronts weakened the originally strong air force.

Other retarding factors

There are more factors which individually would have played almost no role but summed up made an earlier begin of *Barbarous* impossible. Creveld showed that the lacking of equipment and the incomplete training of the German divisions played a major role for the postponement of the attack.[4] Thus the fitting of tanks with air pipes which were necessary for supplying the motors with air while crossing rivers under water had not been finished before early June.[5] The chief of the general staff Halder constantly complained about lacking equipment. The "fast" divisions did not have enough transport trucks. The Gasoline trailers of the tanks were delivered finally in June.[6] Creveld was correct writing: *"It is quite clear that lack of equipment of all kinds would have prevented Barbarous from starting before the end of June even if neither Marita nor 25 had come into the world."*[7]

And there was another decisive factor which prohibited an earlier beginning of the offensive: In December 1941 an order to the army in the east said: *"Als zeitlicher Anhalt kann in Rechnung gestellt werden, dass nach dem Winter normalerweise die Operationsmöglichkeiten für den südlichen Teil der Ostfront schon im April, für den mittleren und nördlichen Teil des Ostgebietes erst Ende Mai, Anfang Juni gegeben sind."*[8] Indeed the German summer offensive in 1942 began on 28 June 1942, the offensive in 1943 (operation Zitadelle) as late as 5 July 1943. The Soviet summer offensive against the German Army Group "middle" (Mitte) began

---

1 Ernst Klink, "Die militärische Konzeption des Krieges gegen die Sowjetunion" in: Militärgeschichtliches Forschungsamt (ed.), *Das Deutsche Reich und der Zweite Weltkrieg*, IV, *Der Angriff auf die Sowjetunion* (Stuttgart: Deutsche Verlagsanstalt, 1983), p. 307 According to him 600 trucks, 40 percent of the planes and a considerable number plane motors and transport and communication units. The losses of the VIIIth Flyer Corps stood heavy losses of the Royal Navy vis-a-vis (9 war ships). Vogel, *op. cit.*, p. 509.

2 Klink, *op. cit.*, pp. 302, 315.

3 Zapantis, *op. cit.*, p. 542 writes that about one third of the German air force took part in the operation against Crete which led to a postponement of Barbarous, but he does give an documentary proof for this. Besides that he committed a serious error by not differing the number of transport and fighting planes. He treats the two air force corpses as one and thus come to totally wrong conclusions.

4 *Ibidem*, p. 174. 40 percent of the German Divisions were equipped with French booty

5 *Ibidem*, p. 173.

6 Hans-Adolf Jacobsen, (ed.), *Generaloberst Halder Kriegstagebuch. Band II, Von der geplanten Landung in England bis zum Beginn des Ostfeldzuges (1.7.1940-21.6.1941)* (Stuttgart: W. Kohlhammer, 1963), pp. 411, 421, 425; Klink, *op. cit.*, p. 262f.

7 *Ibidem*, p. 174.

8 *KTB OKW*, I, p. 1082.

on 22 June 1944.[1] The Soviet offensive in March 1944 does not contradict this, as Zapantis believed,[2] it git into thaw and was scarcely able to move forward because of the mud and therefore was called the "mud offensive".

Zapantis made a great effort to prove that the weather in 1941 would have allowed an earlier beginning of Barbarous in May. He examined the amount of rainfall in Eastern Europe and he water gauge of certain rivers. He overlooked the decisive factor: The thaw and the spring rains caused a mud period similar to the autumn equivalent caused by the autumn rain. Great advances are only possible when the fields have dried or frost began. The same is true with the field airports. In the north and the middle of the front dry fields could be earliest expected the by the second half of June.[3] Napoleon had known this and started his Russian campaign on 22 June.

After the end of the campaign against Greece Hitler asked his chief of staff to explain the time schedule for *Barbarous* . It was decided that the campaign should begin on 22 June though the end of the deployment was two days later and originally the date for the planned attack had been the 26 June.[4] This date was approved by Hitler and was not further changed.[5]

Conclusions

After the successful conclusion of the Balkan campaign Hitler and his generals were in a state of hubris. They had achieved in a few weeks by the blitzkriegs what in WWI had not been achieved in years. At the end of April the C.-in-C. of the army von Brauchitsch was convinced that the war against Russia would last four weeks. After that there would follow mopping up operations and the occupation of the huge space. This arrogant perception was shared by many generals. Hitler played va banque in Russia. General de Guingand commented this dryly: *"It is also not unknown that Planners like to find some suitable excuse when their forecasts do not turn out as expected."*[6]

But when they saw that they had made a miscalculation neither Hitler nor his generals were ready to admit this. They began to search for excuses. Hitler's excuse was Mussolini's attack on Greece which had hindered him to attack a few weeks earlier. For the generals it was the weather or the Balkan campaign. Not one general was ready to admit self-critically that their planning had been wrong, that they had overestimated their own forces. The argument that the war had been lost because of the six weeks was suitable to detract attention from one's own failure and was readily accepted. The six-weeks-myth was the perfect excuse. Creveld is absolutely right writing: *"Behind these views there is not only sloppy scholarship which failed to examine the facts, but also wishful thinking based in part upon considerations that have nothing to do with historiography."*[7]

If the Greeks took over the six-weeks-myth it is fully understandable. It flattered Greek assertiveness to have caused Hitler's defeat in WWII. But this blocks the sight on the real achievement of the Greek people: The Greek army showed the world - as the Finnish forces before - at a moment when everybody believed that the dictators were invincible that successful resistance even of a small people was possible. And the ensuing armed resistance in the Greek mountains showed that the freedom was even more unbowed.

1 Hillgruber, *op. cit.*, p. 506f Anmerkung 28.
2 Zapantis, *op. cit.*, p. 538.
3 Vogel, *op. cit.*, p. 483; Hillgruber, *op. cit.*, p. 507.
4 Hillgruber, *op. cit.*, p. 508.
5 *KTB OKW*, I, p. 401.
6 De Guingand, *op. cit.*, p. 78,
7 Creveld, *Legend*, p. 85.

This resistance was supported by all those progressive forces which were denounced as communist after the war. The civil war between 1946 and 1949 intensified this. In all other European states resistance against the Nazis was a reason to be proud of but in Greece it was condemned as communist. The six-weeks-myth was the ersatz. After 1974 the damning of the resistance decreased but the pride of it is confined to the Left. The conservative camp still denounces it. The six-week-myth is the ersatz. This is especially the case in military circles as the example of Paragioudakis shows. For these circles any doubt of the myth is regarded as an attack on the Greek nation as such and is fought wit all means as I encountered it. For these people the myth is above the constitutional rights of freedom of opinion and the freedom of science. Fortunately in my case the court was ready to respect these freedoms and I was acquitted.

In addition the operation *Marita* had an effect on the course of WWII though on a totally different place. In order to send their totally inadequate help to Greece the British stopped the very successful and promising advance towards Libya. They might have been able to throw the Italians into the sea. In this case there would never hae been a German Africa corps. The free-French forces would certainly have taken over in Tunisia and Algeria. in 1941 the whole southern shore of the Mediterranean would have already been in Allied hands The British supply routes would have been shorter and possibly the Royal Air Force and the Royal Navy might much earlier have bombed Italy out of the war. It is an interesting speculation to ask oneself whether Hitler would have risked to attack Russia if North-Africa was in Allied hands. But the British ruined this chance by enforcing their inadequate help onto Greece. Thus the real help for Greece was not the task but the effect of this help on the American public to achieve the acceptance of the lend-lease program. But this is another story.

THE FAMINE IN WINTER 1941-1942

In the winter of 1941more than 300,000 Greeks died of hunger in Attica

In 1967/68 I was in Athens to do research for my doctoral dissertation on the history of Greece during WWII. During my research in the literature I came across a horrible number: 300,000 Greeks had died of hunger in the winter of 1941. During my earlier studies I had read that during the same winter 1 million inhabitants of Leningrad (St. Petersburg) had died of hunger and that they had been buried in special burial grounds. When I arrived in Athens I asked people where these special burial grounds were. They seemed astonished and told me that such burial grounds did not exist in Attica. People who died of hunger had been buried in normal cemeteries. I had visited some Athenian cemeteries and had seen that they all were not very big. Therefore I came to the conclusion that something was wrong because the capacity of the regular cemeteries could never have been big enough for 300,000 dead.

I looked into the topic and found out that the number of 300,000 is a total exaggeration. After detailed research efforts I found out that the real number is 30,000 and published it in my book on the history of Greece between 1936 and 1946.[1] But my findings have not been acknowledged. Therefore to this day in literature and historical consciousness not only of the Greeks but of the Germans also the number 300,000 has remained. It became the historical truth. As my book in which I presented the correct number has been out of print for many years it seems reasonable to present the facts here once more.

The economic background

68 percent of the Greek territory is mountainious, 32 percent plains but only 30 percent are arable.[2] Sweet-Escott wrote in his classic account: *"Less than a fifth of the area of Greece is cultivated, and the cultivable area can be little greater. From classical times the country has been unable to provide enough food for its people. Thus in terms of value imports of commodities habitually exceed exports by a large margin. This has consequently driven the Greeks to commerce and emigration, and rendered them exceptionally dependent on foreign capital. But the peculiarity of the economic position does not arise merely from Greece's inability even when times are good to produce more than half the wheat and a quarter of the cereals she requires."*[3]

Another reason for the tiny production was the total underdevelopment of Greek agriculture: Until WWII only 1,700 tractors existed, i.e. for 218 peasants there was one tractor (in Bulgaria 221 peasants to one tractor, in Britain it was 3 to 1). The consumption of chemical fertilizers per year and hectare was 75 times smaller than in the Netherlands. Even information about better cultivation methods did not reach the Greek peasants because in 1920 52 percent of them were analphabets.[4] The consequence was that Greece had to import half of her cereals for bread until WWII.[5]

The impact of the war

---

1 Heinz Richter, *Griechenland zwischen Revolution und Konterrevolution (1936-1946)* (Frankfurt: EVA, 1973).

2 *Ibidem*, p. 32f.

3 Bickham Sweet-Escott, *Greece. A Political and Economic Survey 1939-1953* (London: Royal Institute of International Affairs, 1954), p. 9.

4 Leften S. Stavrianos, *The Balkans since 1453* (New York: Holt, Rinehart and Winston, 1965), p. 679.

5 *Ibidem*, p. 678; Marios Nikolinakos, "Materialien zur kapitalistischen Entwicklung Griechenlands (Teil 1)," *Das Argument*, 57 (1970), p. 192f.

The war against the Italians in Albania led to a reduction of the agricultural production. Many peasants were drafted into the army and could not till their fields. Most tractors and 85 percent of the draught animals were needed to transport war material. After the end of the fighting only 150 tractors were given back to their proprietors. These losses were not balanced by the delivery of 100 German tractors after Greece was occupied. Of the 270,000 draught animals only 80,000 were given back to the peasants. The amount of the agricultural production was further reduced by separation of East Macedonia and Western Thrace. But only 13 percent of the Greeks lived in these zones which were occupied by the Bulgarians.

The following statistic shows the wheat production in thousand tons; the number in brackets show the imports:[1]

	production	import
1938	983t	(475t)
1939	1.042t	(366t)
1940	905t	(273t)
1941	566t	-
1942	343t	-

Parallel to the decline of the production there were difficulties with transport. During the fighting many means of transpiration had been destroyed. After the occupation of Greece the occupiers confiscated a lot of the still existing capacity. The Greek merchant marine had fled almost completely which caused a lack of transport ships in the Aegean. The division of the country into three occupation zones also had negative effects on the distribution of the existing foodstuff. The supply situation was made even worse by a law which Metaxas had released during the war and which forbade private household to hold provisions. In WWI the private storage had prevented a similar catastrophe when a blockade was imposed on Greece by the Allies.

The blockade in WWI was proposed by the French who wanted that King Constantine gave up his policy of neutrality. In the beginning the British hesitated to impose a blockade because they knew that it would cause a famine but on 8 December 1916 the blockade was imposed on Greece. The blockade caused a horrible famine especially upon the poor part of the population. Many people died of hunger. The blockade was lifted when the King went into exile and Venizelos took over.[2]

Begin of the Occupation

Therefore already at the time of the German invasion there was a certain shortage of food. Shortly after his arrival in Athens envoy Altenburg warned that there might be a famine. But foreign minister Ribbentrop was of the opinion that this was a problem of the Italians. These however were agrued against the Germans who allegedly had plundered Greece to last shoe-lace. In the middle of June the chief of staff of the 12th Army warned: *"Die Ernährungslage hat sich weiter verschlechtert. Der gesamte Peloponnes, Epirus und die Inseln sind seit*

1 Red Cross, *Ravitaillement de la Grèce pendant l' Occupation 1941-1944 et pendant les premiers cinq mois après la Libération* (Athènes: Société Hellénique d'Editions, 1949), pp. 25, 28. The numbers after 1940 do not contann the values of Western Thrace, Eastern Macedonia and those of the Ionian Islands.

2 On the famine in WWI Heinz A. Richter, *Geschichte Griechenlands im 20. Jahrhundert, Vol. 1, 1900-1939* (Mainz: Rutzen, 2015), pp. 63, 101 and Stratos Dordanas, "Dying of Hunger in Greece. The food war and public opinion on the war (1915-1917)", in: Heinz A. Richter (ed.), *Aspekte neugriechischer Geschichte. Gesammelte Aufsätze* (Wiesbaden: Harrassowitz, 2018), pp. 23-29.

mehreren Wochen ohne Brot, das die Hauptnahrung darstellt. Die Landwirtschaft kann kaum Erzeugnisse bieten. Es fehlt zudem an den Möglichkeiten des Transports und der Erfassung. Es muss befürchtet werden, dass durch eine eintretende Hungersnot Epidemien ausbrechen. Zudem beeinflußt die Ernährungslage sehr stark die Stimmung des Volkes ... Die durch die Ernährungslage bedingte Mißstimmung des Volkes bildet den Nährboden für kommunistische Propaganda. Während zunächst in Athen und Piräus nur Maueranschläge festgestellt wurden, kam es in Nordgriechenland des öfteren zu Überfällen und Plünderungen. Die Polizeigewalt reicht nicht aus, um solche Ausschreitungen zu verhindern ..."[1]

In the literature one often reads that the scarcity of the food had been caused by the Germans. Two examples may illustrate this: In 1959 the British historian Meddlicott wrote in his book about the blockade, that the Wehrmacht had systematically plundered Greece. Primarily foodstuff had been confiscated and sent to the Africa Corps in Libya.[2] Mazower alleges that the German occupants had pressed foodstuffs out of Greece which were sent to the German troops in Libya and Russia. Thus the basic supply of the population had become dubitable.[3]

How the first contention could have been realised in view of the total lack of ships is a mystery. Mazower overlooks two main points: the fact that almost all German troops had been withdrawn immediately after the occupation and that the railway line from Niş to Athens is single track and had been destroyed in several sections How the foodstuffs could have been brought North is his secret.

The often read contention that Germany confiscated foodstuffs is wrong proven by facts. In the final report of the *Commission de Gestion* of the international Red Cross numbers are mentioned which make it clear that the confiscations and handovers had bee confined to traditional export goods such as dried figs, dried grapes and olive oil. In 1940 102,000 tons of olive oil had been produced of which 39,000 tons were exported. In 1941 84,000 tons had been produced of which 10,000 tons were confiscated. However the Red Cross also stated that the producers hesitated to bring their oil to the markets. They scented higher prices on the black market.[4] It is true that fresh vegetables and fruits were transported to Libya by planes, but these were of small quantities and these transports ended soon. Cereals were not confiscated.[5] Documents of the Vatican also prove that the Wehrmacht did not embezzle Greek cereals.[6]

A great part of the confiscated goods even served the Greek people. They were given to the Greek Government so that it could fight the black market. Clever peasant created secret depots in order to achieve higher prices on the black market. How much the black market grew became obvious when the Government Tsolakoglou appointed a new minister of the interior who was to combat the black market with the help of special courts and special police

1 Martin Seckendorf, *Die Okkupationspolitik des deutschen Faschismus in Jugoslawien, Griechenland, Albanien, Italien und Ungarn (1941-1945)* (Heidelberg: Hüthig, 1992), p. 157.

2 William Norton Meddlicott, *The Economic Blockade*, II (London: HMSO, 1959), p. 262.

3 Mark Mazower, *Inside Hitler's Greece. The Experience of Occupation 1941-44* (New Haven: Yale UP, 1993); a totally unchanged German edition appeared in 2016:. Mark Mazower. *Griechenland unter Hitler. Das Leben während der deutschen Besatzung 1941-1944* (Frankfurt: Fischer, 2016).

4 *Ravitaillement*, p. 26.

5 *Ibidem*, p. 31.

6 Hagen Fleischer, *Im Kreuzschatten der Mächte. Griechenland 1941-1944* (Frankfurt: Peter Lang, 1986), p. 119.

which consisted out of incorruptible combatants.[1] The black market flourished. Early resistance groups called for a delivery boycott.

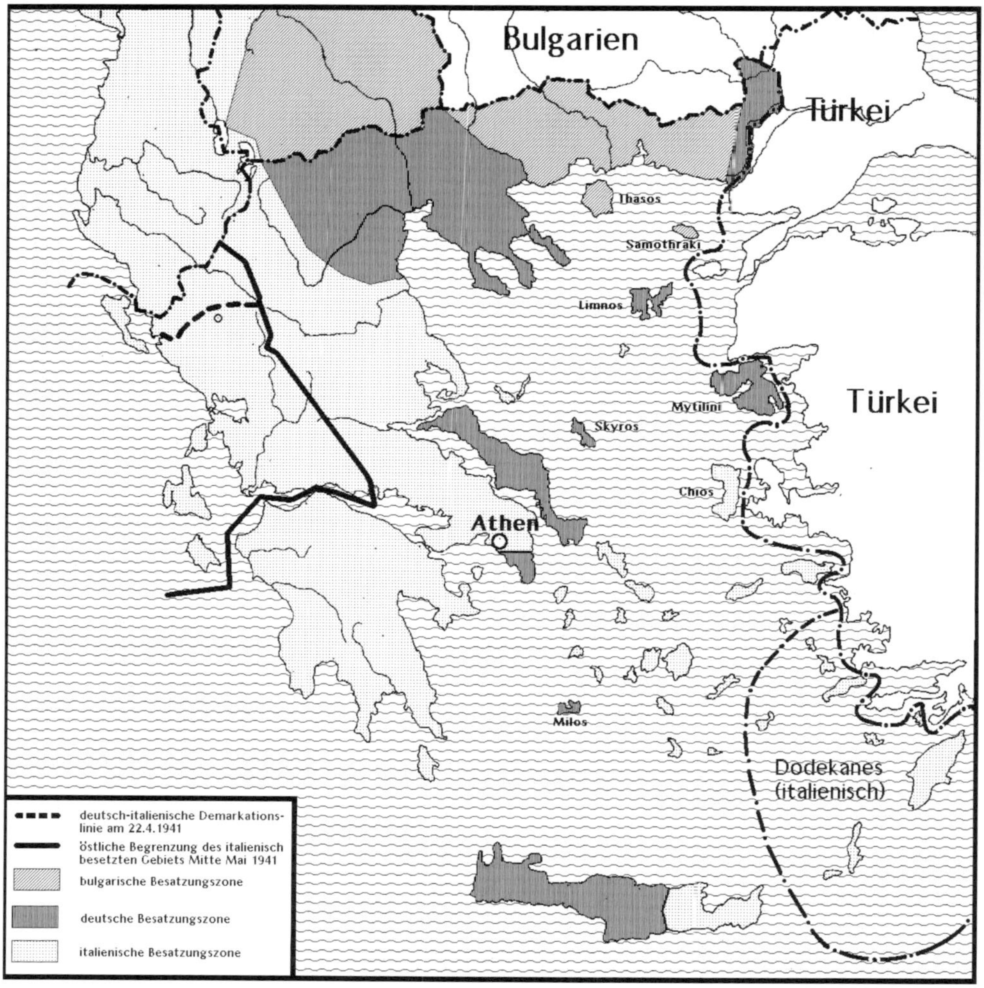

The Occupation Zones

The hunger hit the economically weak urban lower strata. In 1969 the former vice-commander of the EDES resistance group, Komninos Pyromaglou, told me that even during the worst period of the famine it was possible to have a meal *à la carte* in certain feudal restaurants in Kolonaki.

Another grave factor causing the famine was the division of the country. Eastern Macedonia and Western Thrace, important production areas of cereals, had come under Bulgarian rule. Germany controlled the area around Saloniki and strategically important islands (Euboa,

1 C. M. Woodhouse, *Apple of Discord. A Survey of Recent Greek Politics in their International Setting* (London: Hutchinson, 1948), p. 123. The Italian occupation authorities were often not incorruptible and thus fostered the black market.

Milos, Skyros, Chios, Lesbos und Limnos), two thirds of Crete, and a few areas in East-Attica as well as pieces of the Piraeus. The rest of Greece including Athens, was an Italian occupation zone for which Rome was responsible. The occupation of Thrace and Macedonia by the Bulgarians triggered an escape movement. The refugees went to Salonika and Athens where they increased the number of those who had to be fed.

All summer long Altenburg and List tried their best to prevent the threatening catastrophe. The Italian authorities in place also tried their best. They achieved that some cereal was sent to Greece but nether Rome nor Berlin were ready for real help. Though in autumn Italy tried to send more cereal to Greece but Italy herself was suffering of a serious shortage of cereals. Efforts to import cereals from Bulgaria or third countries failed also.

The Blockade

All these factors sharpened the situation but the core problem was the lack of cereal import by the British blockade. When the last British soldiers had left Greece, London imposed a total naval blockade over Greece and cut the country from any outside food supply. Not even the Australian cereals bought and paid for by the Government of Koryzis were allowed to pass through even though it had arrived in Egypt. The British Government was of the opinion that according the Hague Conventions of 1899 and 1907 on war on land, that it was the duty of the conqueror to feed the population of the occupied country.

But the Hague Convention does not say much on this topic. Article 43 demanded that the occupying force was to restore public order and public life if this was possible. Medlicott stated that the British Government was of the opinion that according to the Hague Convention it was the duty of the conqueror to feed the population of the occupied country and give them clothing.[1] But the real aim of the blockade was twofold. The economy of the Axis forces should be weakened. It was believed that the occupied countries were agriculturally self-sufficient. Food supply from neutral countries would extend the war; additionally it could not be controlled and the delivered food supplies should not come into the hands of the Axis powers. Food supply from the outside would stabilize the health of the population and thus their workforce could be used by the occupants. Additionally the food and transport tonnage would be lost for the Allies. Limited supplies would raise false hope and greater demands in the occupied countries.[2]

The second aim of the blockade was to provoke resistance in the occupied countries. Hunger would drive the people into rebellion. The suffering of the people was accepted consciouly. The justification was article 43 of the Hague Convention. Thus all responsibility rested with the Axis Powers.

Mazower prevaricates the causality and trivialises of the blockade when he writes: *"Die Achsenmächte stellten es so dar, als hätten die Briten mit ihrer Seeblockade die Hungersnot verursacht, und schlugen vor, die Blockade solle aufgehoben werden, damit Getreide von außerhalb Europas nach Griechenland gebracht werden könne. Für die Deutschen wäre das eine bequeme Lösung gewesen, aber für die Briten ein schmerzhafter Schritt, denn sie setzten zu einer Zeit auf die Blockade, als sie wenig andere Mittel gegen ihre Gegner zur Verfügung hatten. Hätten die Briten allein zu entscheiden gehabt, ist zweifelhaft, ob die Blockade jemals aufgehoben worden wäre. [...] In Großbritannien und den USA reagierte die Öffentlichkeit empört auf die Hungersnot. Doch erst spät kamen die Briten auf den Gedanken, internationale*

1 Medlicott, *op. cit.*, p. 254.
2 *Ibidem.*

Hilfsanstrengungen für Griechenland zu unterstützen."[1] It is true that the British and American public was critical against the blockade but both Governments had different opinions as we shall see.

The British policy of blockade was not a purely British matter. From the very beginning US Secretary of State Cordell Hull had been one of the strongest supporters, while former President Herbert Hoover was one of the strongest adversaries. The planning and realisation were in the hands of Hugh Dalton the British Minister for economic warfare who also was chief of the SOE (Special Operations Executive). The task of SOE was to provoke and steer resistance in the occupied countries

In March Hull had torpedoed Hoover's plan to send food to Belgium. But a tiny easing of the strict policy of blockade took place in April 1941. Dalton's ministry told the Americans that food deliveries from neutral European countries to occupied ones would be allowed. But the State Department remained on its hard course; only Vichy-France would be excepted.[2] The reasons for Hull's hard course are not fully clear; besides that the US treasury was not ready to provide Dollars for areas inside the blockaded regions.

During the whole summer of 1941 Churchill and Dalton rejected a relief action of te American Red Cross for Belgium. One should not make any concessions. Britain insisted that it was the duty of the Germans to take care of the occupied countries. On 19 July Hull stated that the US pitied the starving peoples but the responsibility for the supply rested with the Axis Powers.[3] On 22 September the State Department told the British that each exception of the blockade would create so many difficulties that the only solution was a strict rejection.

Against Hull's course Hoover organized a campaign in the Senate. Its climax was the publication of a letter by Hoover in which he said that the US was following a policy of hunger and slow death because this was British policy.[4] On 19 October Hoover demanded that the US Government should seek an agreement which permitted the distribution of food under the control of a neutral state. Thus Hoover proceeded even further in view of the hardship in the occupied countries. He was even ready to forgo the control of charitable donations by the US.

On 21 September Hull hardened his course. He told Dalton that not one Dollar should be used for supply of the occupied countries. Thus Hull turned against the little concession which the British had made regarding the supply within the blockade area. This tough attitude influenced the negotiations of the Foreign Office with the Turks about possible supply deliveries to Greece. Dalton also was against this because he wanted to disturb the transportation routes of the occupiers on land. He would allow transport by ship only inside the Aegean for supplies of the islands.

Eden managed to make Dalton revise his position. Ambiguous reasons - probably the pressure of the American public - also made Hull change his opinion. On 13 October the first Turkish ship (*Kurtuluş - Liberation)* with supply goods was sent to Greece flying the flag of the International Red Cross.

On 11 and respectively on 15 November the German and Italian Government made declarations of guarantee to the Red Cross. In these they declared that they agreed to the sending of

1 Mazower, *op. cit.*, p. 70f.
2 Medlicott, *op. cit.*, p. 256.
3 *Ibidem*, p. 258.
4 *Ibidem*.

supply ships and that the food would be used for the Greek population and the ships could return unmolestedly.[1]

The Policy of the Axis Powers

As the German files show the Axis Powers had recognized the supply difficulties. But after the withdrawal of the German troops and the transfer of the occupation on Italy Berlin was of the opinion that the Italians were responsible for the supply.

But the German authorities recognized rather early the problem of the faulty Greek supply and tried to intervene. A memorandum of the director of the politico-economic department of the foreign ministry (AA - Auswärtiges Amt) of 25 July 1941 shows clearly that Altenburg had passed on the urgent request of the Greek Government. But until then Altenburg's appeals had not been considered because in Berlin they were of the opinion that Greece was an Italian affair. Besides that the ministry of supply had categorically rejected any help because of the Reich's food situation. But a little later Carl Clodius would have negotiations about the economic problems with the Government in Rome. One topic would be the Greek situation.[2]

From a reply telegram from Ribbentrop of 18 August it becomes clear that Altenburg had once more brought forward the supply situation on 11 August. In his reply telegram Ribbentrop pointed out that the alliance with Italy preceded any economic consideration regarding Greece.

Parallel to Altenburg's efforts Field Marshall List referred to the critical supply situation of Greece in a message to the AA.[3] In a interministerial conference with the supply ministry on 29 August it was decided in connivance with the Italians that the 10,000 tons of grain of the Banat which were determined for Germany would be sent to Greece. Italy also would send 10,000 tons immediately. In the months October to December 40,000 tons would be sent from the countries of South Eastern Europe. From January to June 1941 each month 15,000 tons would be sent. Primarily these supplies should come from Bulgaria out of the occupied Thrace and from Turkey.[4]

On 15 September 1941 Wiel stated in another memorandum that 5,000 tons were on their way from the Banat to Athens. In the meantime, an Italian supply of 5,000 tons had arrived in Athens. But the situation had changed because Bulgaria had declared that because of its own critical supply situation it could not send grain to Greece. Wiel added that it had been learned from newspapers that an action of the American Red Cross under British tolerance was under preparation to supply Greece with food from Turkey. Ribbentrop needed one week until he declared he saw no reason to supply Greece with food at the cost of an adequate supply of Germany.[5]

The food ministry of the Reich had stated that supplies sent to Greece could take place only at the expense of the German supply. On 12 September it was decided that deliveries of more than the 10,000 tons would have to wait until the compilation of the harvest results by the commission of the Four Years Plan, to be submitted by the end of September. The authorities of the Four Years Plan would then submit a distribution plan for all countries.

---

1 Text of the declaration in: Conrad Roediger, "Die internationale Hilfsaktion für die Bevölkerung Griechenlands im Zweiten Weltkrieg" *Vierteljahreshefte für Zeitgeschichte* 11 (1963), p. 58.

2 Doc. Ger, Pol. XIII, Nr. 155, p. 218f.

3 *Ibidem*, Nr. 323, p. 513; vgl. *Fall 7, Sitzungsprotokolle, p. 6.779.*

4 *Doc. Ger. Pol.*, XIII, Nr. 323, p. 513.

5 This declaration was restricted in the sense that Germany was ready supp y Greece so far that the necessary German imports from there were assured and possible unrests be avoided

On 24 October envoy Eisenlohr composed another memorandum on the supply situation of Greece. He stated that the German and Italian effort to supply Greece with grain from third countries had failed. Therefore at the beginning of October the German embassy had declared to the Italians that in the future Germany would leave the responsibility for supplying Greece to the Italians because Greece was in their sphere of influence. This declaration was to hinder the Italians to demand from Germany to supply Greece with its own supplies. The Italian Government would try to get 100,000 tons of wheat or maze from Bulgaria.

Eisenlohr referred to an order of Hitler according to which the 60,000 Greek workers of the Wehrmacht in the German occupation zone and other Greeks who worked for the Germans were to be supplied with food. Eisenlohr emphasized that Field Marshall List had demanded a monthly delivery of 10,000 to 15,000 tons of cereals until the end of the year.[1]

The end of the development, contained in German diplomatic documents is the telegram from Clodius to Altenburg of 17 November 1941 in which he was stated that it was agreed with Italy that Germany, after the mutual failure to get supplies form Bulgaria, Rumania and Turkey could not participate in a long term plan to supply Greece. Germany however was ready to deliver 10,000 tons of grain until the end of the year to avoid the worst especially in the Piraeus and Athens.[2]

The efforts of the German and Italian governments to send supplies to Greece prove that at least the German authorities in Greece tried to help the population. The Italian Plenipotary Ghigi and his German colleague Altenburg and the C.-in-C. of the Wehrmacht in the Southeast (Wehrmachtsbefehlshaber Südost) List did their best to inform their superiors about the misery in Greece. Quite in contrast to Medlicott's presentation who only refers to the Italian memorandum of the Italian foreign ministry of 7 August 1941and speaks of only one conversation between the Germany and Italy in summer 1941[3] several negotiations took place during which the Italians recognized their responsibility for occupied Greece.[4]

Direct deliveries from Germany and Italy could only solve the immediate hardship. Therefore both countries tried to find help from third countries. If one takes a certain cynicism of the two governments into consideration regarding the fate of the occupied countries this explains a lot of the behaviour of the two governments. Additionally Italy herself was suffering of a lack of breadstuff as is shown by Ciano's diary.[5] In Germany also there was no food abundance in the winter of 1941. All this shows that Italy was conscious of her responsibilities as the main occupation power and tried to fulfill her obligations.

It must be stated here that the commander in Southern Greece (Befehlshaber Süd-Griechenland) Hellmuth Felmy, did his best to fight the hunger in the small zone which he controlled. Felmy's task at that time was to build up the German-Arab units called special unit F, an Arab force which was to be deployed later in the Iraq. Befehlshaber Süd-Griechenland Felmy was only in personal union.[6] In the other areas controlled by the Germans there was no famine. Food was short but there were no hunger deaths.

---

1 *Doc. Ger. Pol.*, XIII, Nr. 420, p. 676ff; Totally Germany delivered 80.000 tons cereals n 1941t. Cf. *Ravitaillement*, p. 33.

2 *Doc. Ger, Pol.*, XIII, p. 679 Fußnote 6.

3 Medlicott, *op. cit.*, p. 266 Fußnote 2.

4 *Doc. Ger. Pol.*XIII, Nr. 501, p. 829.

5 Galazzo Ciano, *Tagebücher 1939-1943* ²(Bern: Scherz, 1947), p. 350.

6 Gerhard Weber, *Hellmuth Felmy. Stationen einer militärischen Karriere. Suez Front - Reichswehr - Luftflotte II - Sonderverband F - LXVIII. Armeekorps in Griechenland - Nürnberger Prozess* (Ruhpolding, Mainz: Rutzen, 2010).

Developments between November 1941 and January 1942
The foodstuff delivered by the *Kurtuluş* was controlled by a central control commission of the IRK (International Red Cross). This commission was active until the big international help action began in 1942. The IRK deliveries from Turkey were transported by *Kurtuluş* and another ship called *Dana*. Between October 1941 and August 1942 these two hips brought 20,000 tons of food from Turkey. Altogether the *Commission de Gestion* distributed 45,000 tons of foodstuff.[1] But all the deliveries which arrived in Greece were scarcely more than the famous drop of water on a hot stone.

During November and December the Vatican mediated new talks between the warring parties. Again the differing legal positions clashed. The British spoke of the obligation of the occupants to supply the occupied .population and the Axis powers denounced the blockade as[2] American dollars a violation of international law. The Vatican stressed the duty of both parties to save human lives. But the stubborn adherence of both sides on legalistic positions led to the famine of the winter of 1941.

The Americans remained on their stubborn position until December 1941 and did not allow any transport of cereals to Greece. After the attack of the Japanese on Pearl Harbour on 7 December 1941 the American ambassador John Winant hinted on 11 December in the Foreign Office in London that the US would agree to certain deliveries.[3] The American entry into the war enabled the US to actively intervene in the war. They were no longer committed to indirect warfare. Moreover the pressure of the American help organisations increased. On 3 January the State Department declared its agreement that American Dollars could be used to buy food in Turkey.[4]

On 12 January 1942 the War Cabinet in London decided to allow the passage of 8,000 tons of wheat to pass the blockade to Greece. Churchill who was in Washington at this point received the message together with an urgent appeal of the Minister of State in Cairo, Oliver Littleton, which was supported by the US. On 13 January Churchill telegraphed his agreement which was supported by the US. On 27 January this decision was announced in the House of Commons but emphasized at the same time that blockade policy remained unchanged.[5]

However it soon became clear that this unique delivery was not enough. Therefore in February negotiations about a solution on a greater scale which soon developed into a greater international help action. Before we turn to this the effect of the famine on the Greek population shall be analysed.

The Effects of the Hunger
The effects of the hunger on the population was increased by the extreme cold of winter 1941. As is shown by statistics of the *Commission de Gestion* those who suffered most were the people of Attica and the inhabitants of the islands. At the height of the famine and the cold in the months from December to March the number of mortality rose three times higher from normal. The value of calories for a worker's family dropped to one third of the value before the war.[6]

---

1 Ravitaillement, p. 45.
2 *FRUS 1942*, II, p. 733.
3 *FRUS 1942*, II, p. 733.
4 Prime Minister Tsouderos' letter to Roosevelt certainly played a role. *FRUS 1941*, II, p. 725f.
5 Medlicott, *op. cit.*, p. 267; *FRUS 1942*, II, p. 729f.
6 *Ravitaillement*, pp. 36 und 38.

The description of the famine in Kedros' book is untenable.[1] He alleges that the mortality was seven times higher than before. The report of the *Commission de Gestion* speaks of three times higher. According to Kedros 300,000 people died of hunger.[2] A number which is totally exaggerated.

Of the 1.088.844 inhabitants of Athens the number who died was 8,896 between September and November, 10,244 from December to February, 13.620 from March to May and 8.849 from June to August. Per 1,000 inhabitants these were these 2,73; 6,19; 4,17 und 2,71 dead. More revealing than these numbers which do not contain monthly comparible numbers of the prewar time is a second summary the basis of which are the inhabitants of 127 places with a total number of inhabitants of 2.294.509 people.

Month	comparative figures 1940/41	figures in winter 1941/42	dead per 1.000 inhabitants 1940/41	1941/42
September	1.907	3.196	0,83	1,39
October	2.052	4.268	0,89	1,86
November	2.473	7.262	1,08	3,16
December	3.372	11.207	1,47	4,88
January	3.251	11.715	1,42	5,11
February	2.798	10.586	1,22	4,61
March	2.906	10.957	1,27	4,78
April	2.811	7.962	1,23	3,47
May	2.590	6.206	1,13	2,70
June	2.664	6.091	1,16	2,65
July	3.092	6.210	1,35	2,71
August	3.201	5.842	1,40	2,54

Thus in the er of 1 in the urban centres, the number who died was around 33.000 people. In the hunger winter the deaths were 91,500. The hunger dead were 56,500. In Athens the number who died during this period 51,600 i.e 34,000 of hunger, provided the number of Athens corresponds with the other urban centres.

The Hunger Dead in Propaganda

In April 1942 the BBC alleged that in Greece there had been 500,000 hunger dead. In Greek post-war literature this number was inflated to 800,000. Thus during the first occupation winter one tenth of the Greek population would have died. When the excitement slowly became less the number shrank to 300,000, a number which to this day has remained as well, even in serious literature outside Greece. The number mentioned by BBC was propaganda and may have been believed by the propagandists. Why this number is held onto is unintelligible. It is not understandable why the federal chairwoman of the German Greek Societies, Dr. S. Skarpelis-Sperk, MP sticks to it though I explained the real facts to her in 1972 in my first book and by Hagen Fleischer in 1986 on the basis of Vatican documents. When I presented the facts to her when we were cooperating preparing the book on a conference on Greece in

1 André Kedros, *La Résistance Grecque (1940-1944)* (Paris: Laffont, 1966), p. 77f. His account is based on Dimitrios Gatopoulos, "I martyriki zoi tis sklavias stin Athina" *Istorikon Archeion Ethnikis Antstaseos*, 7 (1958), p. 59ff. Auch diese Darstellung ist voller Fehler.

2 Kedros, *op. cit.*, p. 82.

WWII,[1] she wiped my arguments away and remained at the 300,000 number. When I insisted she terminated our friendship. Fact is that in winter 1941 35,000 people died of hunger in Attica and in all Greece 91,000. Exaggerations damage the truth and the truth is horrible enough in this case.

The International Relief Action

The exceptional permission to send only once 8,000 tons of wheat caused the Greek Government in exile to bombard the responsible British and American authorities with letters demanding the permission of more deliveries.[2] King George directed an urgent appeal to President Roosevelt [3] and Prime Minister Tsouderos threatened to resign.[4]

Blockade minister Dalton who in the meantime had been informed about the existence of armed resistance groups submitted a proposal to the Cabinet which accepted it on 16 February 1942; it had proposed further shipments of cereals and flour to Greece. The transport should be made on ships of neutral states which would have free conduct. One would try to win Sweden for this purpose.[5] The Foreign Office formulated the proposal and on 22 February informed the State Department. According to the plan 15,000 tons of cereals should be shipped each month. Sweden was to submit to the Axis powers the condition that all forces should guarantee free escort to the Swedish ships. The delivered goods would only be distributed to the Greek population. Greek food would be confined to Greeks only and the foodstuffs confiscated by the occupiers should be replaced. The control commission should have full authority and jurisdiction.[6]

In 26 February 1942 the US agreed.[7] On 2 March the British and American envoys, in Sweden, Mallet and Johnson, contacted the responsible member of the Swedish foreign ministry, Erik Boheman. Sweden reacted in a positive way.[8] Boheman assured that Sweden would allocate the necessary ships and would contact the Axis Powers. On British desire the whole affair was camouflaged as a Swedish idea.[9] On 6 March 1942 Boheman declared the definite readiness of his Government to provide the necessary ships and to take over the cost of the commission. The Swedish diplomat Sven Allard would be suggested to the Axis Powers as headman of the Commission. He was qualified and was persona grata with the Germans.[10] On 16 and respectively on 19 March the Swedish envoys in Rome and Berlin spoke to the foreign ministries. Both sides promised to examine the proposals immediately.[11]

During the following weeks the proposals were examined by the competent authorities in the Italian and German Governments. On 2 April the AA gave an intermediate reply.[12] On 15 April the Italian reply arrived in the Swedish foreign ministry. The Italians agreed to the

---

1 Karl Giebeler, Heinz A. Richter, Reinhard Stupperich (eds.), *Versöhnung ohne Wahrheit? Deutsche Kriegsverbrechen in Griechenland im Zweiten Weltkrieg. Beiträge einer Tagung am 27.-28. Oktober 2000 in der Evangelischen Akademie Bad Boll* (Mannheim, Möhnesee: Bibliopolis, 2001) = *PELEUS* Volume 8.
2 Immanouil Tsouderos, *O Episitismos 1941-1944* (Athen: Papazisis, 1946), p. 183ff.
3 *FRUS 1942*, II, p. 736.
4 *Ibidem*, p. 739.
5 Medlicott, *op. cit.*, p. 268.
6 *FRUS 1942*, II, p. 739f.
7 *Ibidem*, p. 743.
8 *Ibidem*, p. 744.
9 *Ibidem,* p. 745 und Roediger, *op. cit.*, p. 59.
10 *Ibidem*, p. 745f.
11 Ciano, *op. cit.*, p. 417 und *FRUS 1942*, II, p. 750.
12 Redigier, *op. cit.*, p. 59.

proposal under the condition that instead of a neutral Swedish control commission the supervision should be made by the IRK (International Red Cross)[1]

Boheman understood that the Italian reservations were a question of prestige and suggested a compromise. A mixed committee should be formed out of members of the IRK and the Swedish Red Cross. Johnson and Mallet agreed.[2] The German reply took some time because Ribbentrop did not want to give an opinion and had given Staatssekretär Ernst von Weizsäcker the task to reply.[3] On 119 April a statement of the British Government was read to the House of Commons in which the readiness of the British was declared to agree to a monthly delivery of 15,000 tons of cereals to Greece. The transport would take place under the supervision of the IRK.[4] This met the concerns of the Italians. On 28 April the German reply was given which accepted the original British plan in its entirety. The new commission was to cooperate with the one already active in Greece.[5]

Boheman, Johnson and Mallet did not agree with this reply.[6] Boheman declared Sweden would try to make Italy change her opinion. But before the German reply arrived in stockholm the position of the IRK became known. The Swiss headman of the IRK Commission, Brunel, had himself commented. He declared that the commission in Greece was unusually dependent upon the occupation forces because of the lack of transport means. The cooperation with the German and Italian Red Cross had proved to be very valuable and irreplaceable because only in cooperation with the occupying armies the necessary transport means could be obtained. Without this cooperation with the occupying forces a relief action would be impossible. Therefore no new commission should be formed but the existing one should be reinforced by Swedes.[7]

Finally on 10 June the IRK achieved by direct negotiations with Rome, the Italian consent to the compromise proposal according to which the existing IRK Committee size should be increased by representatives of the Swiss and Swedish Red Cross.[8]

Boheman said in a conversation with Mallet and Johnson that even the modified version corresponded fully with the original British. Both Governments should agree as quickly as possible to the IRK compromise so that work could begin.[9]

On 13 June 1942 Cordell Hull agreed to the compromise provided the British Government also agreed,[10] which wanted to clear out some concerns.[11] On 7 August the first Swedish ships loaded with Canadian wheat left the harbour of Montreal.

Thus after many months of most difficult negotiations across the fronts a possibility had been found to aid the hungering Greeks. During the following years until the German withdrawal in October 1944 this agreement was enlarged several time. Except for a few tiny conflicts the aid action for Greece functioned smoothly. Both sides correctly adhered to the agreement. The final report of the Commission de Gestion states: "*Abstraction faite des tendances qui se manifestaient auprès des Italiens pendant les premiers six mois de l'activité de la Commission et des abus dont les troupes allemandes se rendaient quelquefois coupables*

1 *FRUS 1942*, II, p. 753.
2 *Ibidem*, p. 755.
3 Redigier, *op. cit.*, p. 61.
4 *FRUS 1942*, II, p. 756.
5 Redigier, *op. cit.*, p. 61; incorrect Medlicott, *op. cit.*, p. 269.
6 *FRUS 1942*, II, p. 758.
7 *Ibidem.*
8 *Ibidem*, p. 761.
9 *Ibidem*, p. 763.
10 *Ibidem*, p. 765.
11 *Ibidem*, p. 768f

vers la fin de l'occupation, on doit reconnaître que les occupants, Italiens aussi bien qu'Allemands, se sont, avec peu d'exceptions, comportés d'une façon correcte envers la Commission. Auprès de quelques hauts fonctionnaires, italiens et allemands, ainsi que chez certains officiers supérieurs et chez un grand nombre de commandants de place, la Commission a trouvé une vrai compréhension de son oeuvre et un désir manifeste d'aider à aplanir les difficultés auxquelles elle se heurtait, évidemment toujours dans la mesure où l'état de guerre le permettait."[1]

Between 1 September 1942 and 20 March 1945 423,274,6 tons of food were sent to Greece. Of these 610,024,3 tons reached Greece. The table gives an overview of the delivered supplies of the years 1942 to 1945.[2]

Year		Wheat	Dried vegetables	Powdered Milk	other Food	Total
1942	Sept.-Dec.	71.030,2	3.047	77,3	88,4	74.242,9
1943	Jan.-March	29.069,6	8.568,9	880,9	-	38.519,4
	April-June	40.357,5	9.337,9	1.069,9	-	50.765,3
	July-Sept.	34.912,6	2.788,7	1.373,6	-	59.074,9
	Oct.-Dec.	54.005,1	12.014, 2	2.573,1	380,8	68.973,2
1944	Jan.-March	43.899,2	4.079,2	937,5	2.316,5	51.232,6
	April-June	66.950,2	17.159,2	2.934,3	5.153,2	92.197.1
	July-Sept.	64.980,4	19.237,2	1.176,5	6.896,5	92.290,6
	Oct.-Dec.	36.492,5	6.027,9	769,1	6.683,0	49.972,5
1945	Jan.-March	21.907,3	17.086,7	2.133,3	13.213,0	54.340,3
Total		463.604,8	99.346,7	13.925,4	34.731,4	611.608,8

The cost for the transport (1 million Dollar per month) was paid by the Greek Government in exile. But already in winter 1942 the financial means of the Greek Government were exhausted and the American Greek War Relief Association subsidized the Government for some time. When its means became scarce the Greek Government appealed to the American government.[3] Thereupon Roosevelt decided that the US would take over the cost of the Swedish ships in the context of the lend-lease regulation.[4]

Conclusions

At the end of this study it seems clear that the contention is no longer true that the Germans have the exclusive responsibility for the famine in Greece in winter 1941/42 because they violated the Hague Convention by not supplying Greece with food. The reasons for the famine are manifold. The British blockade triggered it. Since WWI the British knew that a blockade would cause a famine in Greece. In the first case the British tried to make the Greeks change their policy towards the Entente. In WWII the aim was totally different: The economy of the Axis Powers should be weakened and armed resistance should be provoked. Britain waged a war against Germany and Italy but not against Greece with which it was quasi allied. It took the whole Greek civil population as a hostage to harm its war opponents. Strictly speaking London treated Greece as a war enemy.

The division of Greece into occupation zones sharpened the consequences of the blockade. Italy was the main occupation power and was responsible for the areas occupied by it. Italy

1 *Ravitaillement*, p. 84.
2 *Ibidem*, 239.
3 *FRUS 1943*, IV, p. 167f.
4 *Ibidem*.

could not attend to its duties and did not do enough to get cereals from the Balkan states for Greece. Berlin took the position that Greece was Italy's responsibility. It supplied the small German occupations zones with foodstuff so that there no famine occurred. But none was ready to do something to avoid the big catastrophe. It can be assumed that if Berlin would have really put pressure on the Balkan states they would have delivered. But Berlin was not ready to do this. Thus it can be said that Berlin is as guilty as Rome and London for the famine. And the Greeks became the victims of the war between Britain and the Axis Powers.

As in Greek consciousness the British were allies one could not blame them for the famine, but rather the Germans, not even the Italians. After all, the Germans were responsible for everything which happened after the Italians change of sides in 1943.

THE WAR CRIMINAL MAX MERTEN

The Merten Case

To this day Merten is considered as the greatest war criminal who terrorized Greece during WWII. An article in Ta Nea of 8 October 2005 reported that he had been a close friend of Hitler. Other journalists wrote that he had been an SS-officer who independently organized the destruction the Jews of Salonika. Before he did this, he allegedly promised the Jews of Salonika that he would save them from the annihilation and therefore he was given a huge treasure of golden coins and bullions, diamonds and jewellery, altogether worth 600 million dollars. In 1943 he let this treasure sink at the southern coast of the Peloponnese. The journalists copied their news from one another and each added a new invention. The climax came in 2000 when in the presence of a TV team divers searched for weeks after Merten's treasures. However, what is reality and what is hybrid phantasy of this stories?

Merten's career

Merten was born in Berlin on 8 September 19011. After finishing the Gymnasium he studied law at the university of Berlin. In 1933 he passed the first state exam and 1936 the second. In January 1938 he became a legal assessor and in June 1939 he became a judicial employee in the Ministry of Justice of the Reich. In May 1937 he became a member of NsdAP (Nazi party). Because he suffered from a sport injury he was not called to regular military service but was drafted as an anti aircraft gunner. As he was only able to do office jobs he was transferred to an air force at Berlin-Dahlem as a clerk At the end of 1942 he was made war administrator (Kriegsverwaltungsrat) and his transfer to the Commander Saloniki-Ägäis where as a captain he took over the department of "Administration and Economy".

The Commander Saloniki-Ägäis (until the end of 1942 General Krenzki) was under the command of Wehrmachtsbefehlshaber Südost, List, who was chief of the army command 12. Under his command were the commander Südgriechenland (Felmy) in Athens and the commander of the fortress Crete (until autumn Andrae, then Bräuer), In January 1943 everything was reorganized. We will come back to this.

Until March 1944 Merten remained in Salonika. Afterwards he shortly stayed in Montenegro and Belgrade and later at Tirana from where he moved north with the retreating troops. Until the capitulation in May 1945 he served in the command of the Army Group E in Zagreb. Until the end of 1946 he was a prisoner of war of the Americans and then a civilian internee in Dachau because of his administrative activity in Greece.[1] The Americans offered him to the Greeks as a potential war criminal but the responsible Greek commissioner, General Thomas Ypsilantis did not show any interest; but quite the contrary he pleaded for a quick release because Merten had behaved blamelessly in Saloniki.[2]

---

1 Wolfgang Breyer, *Dr. Max Merten - ein Militärbeamter der deutschen Wehrmacht im Spannungsfeld zwischen Legende und Wahrheit*, Diss. (Mannheim, 2003), p. 12f; Testimony of Merten to Amtsgericht Tiergarten Abt. 353 AR1680/61 on 29 Mai 1961.

2 "Griechenland Beziehungen. Die Falle der Fahndung" *Der Spiegel* 21 (22. Mai 1957), p. 15; Samuel Hassid, "The Trial of Max Merten in the Changing Mirros of Time and Place", in: http://greece.haifa.ac.il/events/holocaust_greece/Samuel_Hassid.pdf; Susanne-Sophia Spiliotis, *Der Fall Merten, Athen 1959: Ein Kriegsverbrecherprozeß im Spannungsfeld von Wiedergutmachungs- und Wirtschaftspolitik* MA-Thesis (München, 1991), p.

After his release from Dachau Merten addressed himself to Greek military mission under Ypsilantis and offered to inform the Greek Government about his activities in Northern Greece during the war. The war crimes office (Grafeio Enklimaton Polemou) in Athens appreciated this, and on 13 January 1947 proposed that Merten should give testimony to the military mission in Berlin. But this meeting did not take place.[1] Merten was not on any allied list of war criminals and in September 1948 the de-nazification (Entnazifizierung) tribunal put him in the category unburdened. Ypsilantis had assured the tribunal *"dass keine Klage von Seiten Griechenlands ... gegen ihn (Merten) erhoben wurde. Im Gegenteil, es sind uns Berichte über sein gutes Verhalten zugegangen. Falls erforderlich, können wir aus Griechenland nähere Nachrichten über ihn einholen."* [2]

Thus it may be stated here that no Greek Government rose any accusations immediately after the war against Merten. However the "National Office for War Crimes had Merten on its wanted list since 1946.[3] But this did not mean much. Fleischer accurately described the status of this list: *"Die Listen enthalten zahlreiche Doppelnennungen, Dutzendnamen (Müller etc.) oder auch nur Vornamen ohne weitere Angaben. Andere Gesuchte werden lediglich mit Dienstrang ('Feldwebel') oder mit verstümmeltem Namen (z. B: Rawglssf) 'identifiziert'. Darüber hinaus sind etwa alle namentlich bekannt gewordenen Mitglieder der Gesandtschaft und der Generalität pauschal erfaßt, oft ohne jeglichen konkreten Tatvorwurf. Die gleichen Einwände gelten für die z. T. identischen Listen, die der griechische Staat 1965 der deutschen Botschaft übergibt."*[4] Therefore it is not astonishing that Merten got onto the list.

On 6 January 1948 this office asked the Foreign Ministry to file a motion with the Americans in Germany that Merten should be extradited because he was a war criminal. The motion was rejected because of formal mistakes. Besides that the motion came too late because since 1 November 1947 the list had been closed.[5] The real reason for the rejection was a totally different case. In May 1947 General Bruno Bräuer had been executed without the slightest justification. The Western Allied were so deeply shocked that from then on they did not any more surrender any "war criminal" to Greece.[6] In 1948 a preliminary investigation by public prosecution ended with the accusation that Merten had been responsible for the drafting of the Jews for forced labour and the arresting of several people.[7]

According to the files of the Berlin Public Prosecutor in 1950 Merten allegedly applied for the position of German General Consul in Athens,[8] which is not very plausible because

---

58f.

1 Spiliotis, *op. cit.*, p. 57f.

2 Breyer, *op. cit.*, p. 13, p. 59 footnote 170.

3 Spiliotis, *op. cit.*, p. 59 footnote 170.

4 Hagen Fleischer, "Der Neubeginn in den Deutsch-Griechischen Beziehungen nach dem Zweiten Weltkrieg und die 'Bewältigung' der jüngsten Vergangenheit", in: Institute of Balkan Studies (ed.), *Griechenland und die Bundesrepublik Deutschland im Rahmen Nachkriegseuropas* (Thessaloniki: IMXA, 1989), p. 101 footnote 72; The list is printed in *Istorikon Archeion Ethnikis Antistaseos* 25-26 (September-Oktober 1960), pp. 68-89. Merten appears twice; as Mertin Max Λοχαγός (Hauptmann - captain) and as Μέρτεν Μαξ Θεσσαλονίκη Στρατιωτικός (Militär). On the list were also the Generals Hellmut Felmy, Hubert Lanz and Wilhelm Speidel, which had be sentenced in the Nuremberg Trial and had been amnestied by McCloy, and the not amnestied General Wilhelm List, who was released from Landsberg because he was seriously ill. Additionally General Heinrich Kreipe was on list who on 1 March 1944 had taken over the command of the 22nd infantry division in Crete and had been kidnapped eight weeks later.

5 Spiliotis, *op. cit.*, p, 58.

6 Gerhard Weber, "Zu den Generalsprozessen. Unterschiede der Verfahren und Urteile über deutsche Besatzungsgeneräle in Griechenland" *Thetis* 18 (2011), p. 267.

7 Spiliotis, *op. cit.*, p. 60.

8 Hagen Fleischer, "Der Neubeginn in den Deutsch-Griechischen Beziehungen nach dem Zweiten Weltkrieg und

Merten had never been in the diplomatic service and in 1950 he opened a lawyer's office. In 1952 Merten worked in the Ministry of Justice for some time but then he returned to his work as a lawyer. Politically Merten engaged himself in the *Gesamtdeutsche Volkspartei* of Gustav Heinemann which propagated a united demilitarised Germany. In 1957 he flew to Athens to do a business job of a client. Besides that he intended to bear witness in a private legal case of his former chief interpreter Arthur Meißner.[1]

Merten's Arrest

In October 1956 it became known in Athens that Germany had paid 300 million DM reparations which had been disguised as an investment credit. The Greek minister of trade, Panagiotis Papaligouras, addressed himself to the German Embassy and asked for an analogue payment by Germany to Greece.[2] During the same time governmental talks began about the termination of the judicial completion of the crimes committed during the occupation. On 27 November 1956 the Greek Foreign Ministry submitted a memorandum to the German Embassy which stated that an amnesty would be released for all war criminals if the Federal Republic was ready to pay compensations to all war casualties. Thus a junctim had been created between an amnesty and reparations.[3] The AA (Foreign Ministry) and the Ministry of Justice (BMJ) regarded this Greek proposal as another attempt to undermine the London Debt Agreement and therefore rejected it. One should try to avoid the impression, *"dass die Bundesregierung vielleicht bereit sein würde, nach Einstellung der in Griechenland anhängigen Strafverfahren, über die Frage einer Entschädigung mit sich reden zu lassen."*[4]

Public prosecutor, Andreas Tousis, urged the German Embassy. Bonn should make a gesture then one could suspend the prosecution measurements. Ambassador Kordt warned Bonn in early April: The only way out pf the impasse would be the acceptance of the Greek proposal for reparations and to signal readiness for negotiations: *"Die Einbringung eines Amnestiegesetzes, das allein einen Schlußstrich unter dieses Erbe der Vergangenheit setzen kann, wird aber ohne Regelung der Entschädigungsfrage für die Opfer der Straftaten nicht möglich sein."* Unfortunately Kordt's word did not encounter open ears in Bonn and the AA did not react. On 23 April the Federal Ministry of Justice (BMJ) rejected any reparation payments categorically and the Greek threat to start again the persecution measures was not justified. *"Die Einbringung eines Amnestiegesetzes, das allein einen Schlußstrich unter dieses Erbe der Vergangenheit setzen kann, wird aber ohne Regelung der Entschädigungsfrage für die Opfer der Straftaten nicht möglich sein."* Leider fand Kordts Warnung in Bonn keine offenen Ohren und blieb im AA zunächst liegen. Am 23. April lehnte das BMJ jegliche Entschädigungsleistung kategorisch ab und wies die griechische Drohung, die Fahndungsmaßnahmen wieder aufzunehmen, als ungerechtfertigt zurück.[5] Obviously nobody in Bonn could not imagine that the Greeks would act. But one day before the German citizen Max Merten who was on the persecution list had arrived in Athens.

---

die 'Bewältigung' der Jüngsten Vergangenheit," in: Institute of Balkan Studies (ed.), *Griechenland und die Bundesrepublik Deutschland im Rahmen Nachkriegseuropas* (Thessaloniki: IMXA, 1989), p. 97(

1 Meißner had lived in Athens before the war and had worked as an interpreter during the occupation. After the -surrender1945 his property a (a printer's shop) had been confiscated. In the actual trial it should decided whether the confiscation had been justified. "Griechenland Beziehungen. Die Falle der Fahndung" *Der Spiegel* 21 822. (Mai 1957), p. 16.

2 Lazaridou, *op. cit.*, p. 211f.

3 Spiliotis, *op. cit.*, pp. 40-45.

4 *Ibidem*, pp. 46-49.

5 *Ibidem*, pp. 50-54.

Without Merten's arrival in Athens Tousis threats would have been an idle threat because there were no German war criminals in Greece who might have been arrested. Merten's arrival in Athens, however, changed everything. It can be assumed that Merten's readiness to give testimony in the Meißner trial been known to the Greek judiciary and it had been announced to the War Crime Office. And Merten's name was on that list. It was a perfect timing.

On 22 April 1957 Merten flew to Athens and there he passed the passport control without any problem. In order to be on the safe side that nothing would happen if he appeared in court on 23 April Merten went to the German Embassy and spoke to the head of the legal department, Ulrich Scheske, The latter told him that his appearance in court would be totally hazard-free. Thus reassured on 26 April Merten went to the court to make his statement. When he had finished his testimony the judge had him arrested.[1]

The Embassy rather quickly understood that the forthcoming trial against Merten was a pressurising agent to come to a solution of the reparations question. It was hoped that the whole affair would go off without a hitch.[2] On 15 May the Embassy informed the AA that the Greek Government had tried all tricks to get reparation money. On 20 May the AA demanded that the Merten case should be totally separated from the reparations question. The Ministry of Justice (BMJ) suggested to exert pressure on Greece in case Merten was not released. A representative of the AA suggested to issue a travel warning to all those who had been in Greece during WWII. Athens was angry because the Yugoslavs had received reparations. The economic situation of Greece was so disparate that Athens was ready to use every means to get money. The Embassy should be informed that Bonn would not accept any package deal.[3] On 29 April the AA instructed the Embassy to demand the immediate release of Merten and his unhindered departure. The position of the Federal Government in the reparations question was known.[4] On 16 May the Embassy reported to the AA that a suspension of the trial could only be achieved in connection with an arrangement of the reparations question. It was recommended that the AA should examine this benevolently.[5]

On 22 May DER SPIEGEL wrote: *"Die Lösung des Rätsels ist, dass Merten das erste Opfer einer Auseinandersetzung wurde, in deren Verlauf die griechische Regierung seit einem Jahr auf gut balkanische Weise versucht, die Bundesregierung unter Druck zu setzen und sie zu außerplanmäßigen Reparationsleistungen zu veranlassen."*[6] This article and some similar ones caused prosecutor Tousis to angry reactions as is shown by an Embassy report of 3 June: *"Die Art der Behandlung des Themas befremde ihn, vor allem fühle er sich durch den Vorwurf der 'balkanischen Methoden der griechischen Regierung' getroffen."* The German Government should do the same as he had done when he forbade the Greek press to write about the preliminary investigations against Merten. The Embassy told Tousis that the German Government had no means to stop the press report as the Greek press law permitted. The AA was asked why the German press described Merten as a victim. The role of a martyr did not suit Merten.[7]

1 *Ibidem*, p. 56f.
2 Susanne-Sophia Spiliotis, *Der Fall Merten, Athen 1959: Ein Kriegsverbrecherprozeß im Spannungsfeld von Wiedergutmachungs- und Wirtschaftspolitik* MA-Arbeit (München, 1991), p. 64. BA/B 305-1041.
3 Aktenvermerk des DBMdJ 9250/1-3-12562/57 vom 20. Mai 1957. BA B 141/9566, pp. 37-44.
4 BA B 141/9566, p. 51.
5 RK 515-10 Ber. Nr. 533/57 vom 16. Mai 1957 BA B 141/9566, pp. 62-67.
6 "Griechenland Beziehungen. Die Falle der Fahndung" *Der Spiegel* 21 (22. Mai 1957), p. 15.
7 RK 515-10 Ber. Nr. 598(57 vom 3. Juni 1957 BA B 141/9566, pp. 80-81.

The Embassy warned the AA several times. But the AA and the BMJ remained at their position. The latter demanded that the court procedure should be stopped. The Embassy again warned that if no concessions would be made to the Greeks the trial would go through with all awkward accompaniments. But Bonn remained stubborn. There they believed that the Greeks only wanted money.[1]

Then the BMJ tried a trick: The persecution of the war criminals who had been active in Greece had been active in Germany as proof of this the BMJ submitted a list of cases. But it was easy to recognize that this list had been prepared ad hoc because almost all cases carried the date 1957, i.e. the were new cases. Additionally they did not carry the numbers of the files. Schmoller came to the conclusion, *"dass dem BMJ an einer Ermittlung und Bestrafung der Beschuldigten nicht gelegen war."* The Greeks had understood the transfer of the cases in 1952 and 1956 had only had the purpose *"den Fortgang der Verfahren in Griechenland zu hemmen.. [...] Meines Erachtens haben wir hier keine Forderungen zu stellen. Deutsche haben in Griechenland Straftaten begangen und der Strafanspruch des griechischen Staates ist ebensowenig verjährt wie die Erinnerung des Volkes an die Leiden der Besatzungszeit gelöscht ist. Wenn die griechische Regierung einen Vorschlag zur Lösung des Problems vorlegt, so wäre ich im Interesse unserer Gesamtbeziehungen dankbar, wenn er geprüft wird, zumal die griechische Seite in der bisherigen Behandlung der Verfahren im Rahmen des Gesetzes wirklich bis an die Grenze des Möglichen gegangen ist."*[2]

Bonn, however, was not ready to give in. The AA looked for honest witnesses for the defence and developed a slightly abstruse ideas. The Siemens Company should be addressed about Dimitrios Makris who had been its local lawyer during the occupation and was now Minister of Justice.[3] However after the exchange of more messages between the Embassy in Athens and the AA in Bonn it became clear that Bonn had to move.

The first proposal showed that Bonn had not grasped the real matter. One was ready to start a trial against Merten in Germany. For this purpose Merten should be transferred to Germany for interrogation while Greece would tacitly accept that he would not return.[4] Obviously it was not understood in Bonn that such games were excluded in the meantime. Nevertheless AA and BMJ decided to send the former chief of the German delegation, Ernst Kanter, who had led the negotiations in 1952 and 1956 to Athens with the mission to find a solution.

On 25 July Kanter and Tousis met. Kanter "proved" that war criminals were punished in Germany. He even alleged that a procedure had been opened against Merten. But this procedure did not progress because Merten was in Greece in jail. Kanter proposed a extradition. Tousis rejected this because Merten had committed his crimes in Greece and was in court there. The court responsible for his case would reject any extradition. However, he and the Government were interested in a quick settlement without a trial. As soon as the preliminary investigation were concluded the press could no longer be restrained. *"Daher sei es ratsam, die Frage der Bereinigung des Verfahrens (gegebenenfalls durch Auslieferung oder Überstellung) bald zu klären. Die Lösung sei aber keine Sache der Justiz, sondern der politischen Instanzen."* Tousis then spoke about reparations. Reparations would be the best possibility for a detente. *"Es dürfe nicht so aufgefasst werden, als ob die griechische Regierung den Fall Merten zu einem Handelsobjekt mache und etwa ein Lösegeld herausschlagen wolle."* But the

1 Spiliotis, *op. cit.*, p. 71.
2 Schmoller an AA am 27. Mai 1957: BA/ZWA B 141/9566, p. 56, zit. n. Spiliotis, *op. cit.*, p. 75f.
3 Spiliotis, *op. cit.*, p. 77.
4 *Ibidem*, p. 83.

proposal should be examined. *"Im übrigen werde nach seiner Auffassung und auch nach Auffassung der zuständigen Regierungsstellen ein verhältnismäßig kleiner Garantiefonds genügen. Es sei lediglich an eine symbolische Abfindung gedacht."*[1]

Several times Tousis assured that *"nicht etwa eine Erpressung mit Lösegeld beabsichtigt sei."* Kanter came to the conclusion that Germany had not behaved in the proper way in the past. *"Wir haben es Griechenland sehr schwer gemacht, uns in der Kriegsverbrecherfrage entgegenkommend zu behandeln. Wir haben den Griechen trotz mehrfacher mündlicher Anfragen nicht mitgeteilt, wie es mit der Einleitung unserer Verfahren stehe."* The initiated criminal proceedings should be expedited quickly so the impression created in Greece of a casual execution should be dispersed. The Greek side should be informed that they could end the parallel cases in Greece. Additionally a political solution should be aspired.[2]

On 17 October the German minister of justice resignedly stated that the Merten case could not be solved by judicial means. One had to talk about reparations. Only by this could something be accomplished. Tough this did not agree with the London Agreement it was the only way to overcome the Greek-German tensions.[3]

The AA however rejected the Greek demand for reparations. The Embassy should insist on the transfer of Merten or demand a speedy trial. The AA was afraid hat the Greek Government would postpone the trial out of fear of a battle with the opposition in the press. Therefore Merten would remain in jail without any trial. At the same time the central legal protection department of the AA was to find exonerating evidence for the defence of Merten.[4]

On 15 March 1958 the Greek Government gave a memorandum to the German Embassy in which it again proposed reparations as a solution for the whole war criminal problem. Though the Greek Government knew that Germany rejected this it assured it of further readiness for cooperation. Though the Government did not have any influence on the judiciary it promised an early act of grace if he were convicted. But the AA continued to try to free Merten without making any concession in the reparation question. The AA developed the idea that Federal President Heuss might appeal to King Paul. The Greek side also began to think about how to liquidate the case somewhat quietly. But all this did not lead anywhere because at the end of March the chamber responsible for war criminal cases decided to transfer the Merten case to a special military court. This decision was taken because a military court could be controlled by the Government. Additionally a military court was not obliged to check the truth of the statements of witnesses for the defence, or of the prosecution.

With this decision the box of Pandora was opened because from now on the press and the left EDA party could participate. The Merten case became the vehicle of the opposition against the conservative Government of Karamanlis. Because the atmosphere in Greece was heating any deportation was excluded. Because of the internal political mudslinging even a death penalty was threatening Merten. Resigning Ambassador Kordt stated that one could not stop developments.[5] One can speculate whether without the weak interim Government Tousis would have dared to take this decisive step.

In Bonn the AA had brought itself to making a new offer to the Greeks. One would inform the Greek Government that the pre-trial proceedings against Merten would be speeded up and thus the main trial would occur soon. Thus an extradition of Merten would be possible for the

1 Memo on the conversation with Tousis on 25 July 1947. BA B 141/9566, pp. 141-143.
2 Memo on Kanter's trip of 7 August 1957: BA B 141/9566, pp. 152-157.
3 Letter Merkatz to Brentano on 17 Oktober 1957: BA B 141/9566, pp. 204-206
4 Spiliotis, *op. cit.*, p. 96f.
5 *Ibidem*, pp. 98-101.

Greek side. At the same time it would be signalled to the Greeks that, if they assured to transfer Merten sooner or later, an economic delegation could be sent to Bonn to talk about economic support. By this it became clear that Bonn accepted a link between the Merten case and the economic aid: *"Die von griechischer Seite angestrebte deutsche Wirtshaftshilfe verstärkt unsere Position. Die deutsche Botschaft wird beim Außenminister in Griechenland vorsichtig durchblicken lassen, dass es in der deutschen Öffentlichkeit nicht verstanden würde, wenn solche Verhandlungen vor der Regelung des Falles Merten stattfänden."*[1] These indications were made and a little later the release of a special law for war criminals was announced. It was a signal towards Bonn. Obviously new talks were wanted to avoid further damage of the bilateral relations.

Tousis behaviour regarding the compensation of the Jewish Greeks was most astonishing. If the claims for damages of the Greeks were compensated a legal amnesty solution could include Merten. The enforcement of damage claims of the Jew Tousis considered futile. This attitude was not understood by the German side since the EDA made great fuss about this question. Most probably Tousis blocked this reparations demand because it was pressed by the left. It is possible, however, that he assumed that a purely Greek reparation payment could be obtained more easily because the Jewish demand comprised many western states and was much larger. But it should be noted here, that Tousis was only interested in pushing through the Greek demands.[2]

In the meantime the Greek manhunt machinery went full speed. In mid-June 1958 Schmoller, councillor of the German Embassy complained in the Greek Foreign Ministry that *"in letzter Zeit immer wieder deutsche Staatsangehörige, die entweder als Touristen nach Griechenland kommen oder sich hier ständig aufhalten, unter dem Verdacht, in Griechenland Kriegsverbrechen begangen zu haben, Vorladungen von der Polizei erhalten oder von dieser gesucht werden."* The report of the embassy added that Tousis was trying to build up additional pressure *"um die deutsche Seite für seinen Vorschlag geneigter zu machen, Verhandlungen über die Frage der Zahlung von Entschädigungen aufzunehmen."* These measure were only directed against innocent people because criminal proceedings had been set in motion in Germany. These people were warned and would certainly not travel to Greece. If these persecutions went on a general travel warning should be issued.[3]

In the middle of July it became known in Bonn that Tousis intended to spend his holidays in Germany and wanted to have a talk in Bonn. The AA agreed that he should be received but that the talks would have a totally private character.[4] On 30 July a first meeting took place in the BMJ (Ministry of Justice). Tousis stressed that the purpose of his visit was to get in contact with the appropriate authorities, *"um gemeinsam einen Weg zur Lösung der bestehenden Schwierigkeiten zu finden."* He proposed official talks. His interlocutor replied that he would have to contact his superiors.[5] During his conversation in the AA Tousis stressed that the Greek Government would not use the Merten case to put pressure on the German side in the reparations question. The representative of the AA countered that the Merten case created a headache in Germany and strained the prosperous cooperation. The Federal Government would make an effort in autumn *"Griechenland wirtschaftlich in besonderem Maße unter die Arme zu greifen. Es sei daher schlecht, wenn Hand in Hand mit den von uns beabsichtigten*

1 AA (Ref. 503) - Memo of 22 May 1958: BA/B 305-1047. Quoted from. Spiliotis, *op. cit.*, p. 103.
2 Spiliotis, *op. cit.*, pp. 105-108.
3 BdBRD - SE - 204 Merten Ber. No. 608/58 of 14 June 1958: BA B141/9568, p. 13f.
4 DBMdJ 9250/1-3-23292/58 on 23 July 1958; BA B141/9568, p. 33.
5 DBMJ 9250/1-G on 30 July 1958: BA B141/9568, p. 38.

Maßnahmen, in Athen ein Verfahren angestrebt würde, das drüben wie bei uns zweifellos die öffentliche Meinung in Wallung bringen würde und Reminiszenzen an eine Zeit hervorkehren würde, die von beiden Seiten sicherlich nicht gewünscht würden." The AA asked Tousis to consider whether the declaration of economic cooperation should cause a declaration of a general amnesty. Tousis, however, did not understand that the promise to help Greece economically was exactly that what he wanted only under a different denomination. He remained at his position and added threateningly that the Greek judges could not defy the law.[1] At the end Tousis gave to understand that the trial against Merten would begin in November or December.[2]

When in the middle of September the negotiations about the credits (reparations= began it became clear that the Merten case strained the negotiations. On 10 November Karamanlis arrived in Bonn. The legal department of the AA had proposed that Chancellor Adenauer should hint that the German Government expected a transfer of Merten.[3] On 12 November Adenauer and Karamanlis talked among other things also *"über die griechischen Fahndungsmaßnahmen gegen angebliche deutsche Kriegsverbrecher und insbesondere über den Fall Merten."* Adenauer pointed to the actions of the Greek police against German tourists. Karamanlis declared *"dass er nach seiner Rückkehr nach Athen sich selbst um die Angelegenheit kümmern werde und alles tun werde, um weitere Störungen der deutsch-griechischen Beziehungen zu vermeiden."*[4] On 13 November 1958 a confidential protocol was signed in which the questions of the German war criminals and of the German properties in Greece were regulated.[5]

It is interesting in this context that Konstantinos Svolopoulos in his edition of the archives of Karamanlis described the Bonn visit in detail and wrote about the credit of 200 million DM but also the Merten case is not mentioned with one word. The index of names of this many volume edition does not contain the name of Merten.[6]

After his return to Athens Karamanlis ordered Foreign Minister, E. Averof. and the Minister in the Office of the Prime Minister, K. Tsatsos, to inform the German Embassy that the Merten case was finished by a special law and Merten himself would be transferred to the Federal Republic of Germany. At the end of November it was heard in the News that the persecution of the war criminals had been stopped.[7] This declaration triggered a storm of protest in the Greek press. From *Estia* which was close to Markezinis to the EDA paper *Avgi*, even *Kathimerini* which was friendly to the Government, all papers were united in the rejection. On 2 December 1958 *Eleftheria* wrote that it would be unacceptable that persons who were on trial should be transferred to Germany. This would insult the national dignity.[8]

In January 1959 Karamanlis repeated his promise to Ambassador Kordt that the Merten case would be rectified by an act of grace,[9] but it was clear that the internal Greek pressure was increasing. During a conversation with the new German Ambassador Seelos Karamanlis regretted that he could not keep his promise in the Merten case. The opposition in the cabinet

---

1 Spiliotis, *op. cit.*, p. 109.
2 *Ibidem*, p. 118.
3 Lazaridou, *op. cit.*, p. 257.
4 DBMJ -9250/1-3-23428/58 vom 18. November 1958: BA B 141/9568, p. 137f.
5 Seelos to AA on 11 December 1958: BA/ZWA B 141/9573, p. 26. Quoted from. Spiliotis, *op. cit.*, p. 120.
6 Konstantinos Svolopoulos (ed.), *Konstantinos Karamanlis. Archeio gegonota kai keimena,* Vol. III, *Oktaetia dimiourgias 1956-1963* (Athen: Idryma Konstantinos Karamanlis, 1994), pp. 271-302.
7 Spiliotis, *op. cit.*, p. 120.
8 Anlage zum Botschaftsbericht vom 4. Dezember 1958: BA B 141/9573, p. 30f.
9 Aide Mémoire vom 4. Februar 1959: BA B 141/9568, p. 137f.

was so strong that he could not realize his plan simply to deport Merten to Germany. The trial had to be brought to a finish. He intended for it to have it begun soon and would try to influence the composition of the court to avoid a death sentence. After the judgement Merten would be deported as soon as possible. The German Government should not worry about the other 850 war crime cases.[1]

On 14 January 1959 the Greek Government submitted a draft law about the suspension of the persecution of war criminals which on 29 January was approved by parliament and was signed by the King on 18 February. It read: *"Nachdem die Strafverfolgung deutscher Staatsangehöriger, die als Kriegsverbrecher geführt werden, seitens der Justizbehörden ihres Heimatlandes begonnen hat, wird die Strafverfolgung in Griechenland ausgesetzt (suspendiert), [...] ausgenommen diejenigen Fälle, bei denen die Angeklagten in Griechenland verwahrt werden und gegen dieselben bis zum Inkrafttreten dieses Gesetzes Verweisungsbeschlüsse [...] erlassen worden sind."*[2] Thus Merten could be brought to the court. He was the only defendant who was in a Greek prison. However the German Embassy and the AA realized that the formulation of the suspension was so vague that it was possible to continue arresting people. At the same time it was stated that the *"griechische Regierung bemüht sei, den Vorwurf zu entkräften, dass ein Zusammenhang zwischen der Behandlung der Kriegsverbrecherfrage und den deutschen Krediten besteht."* [3]

In early February it was suspected that Tousis had had his fingers in the game.[4] On 4 February the Embassy detected that Germany had been outwitted because on 5 November 1958 a second case had been opened against Merten which was not covered by the new law. The trial would begin on 11 February 1959. Thus *"die Einhaltung des Bundeskanzler Adenauer am 12. November 1958 in Bonn von dem Ministerpräsidenten [Karamanlis] gegebenen und im Januar dem deutschen Botschafter gegenüber wiederholten Versprechen, dass nämlich der Fall Merten nach der Verurteilung durch einen Gnadenakt bereinigt werden würde, praktisch unmöglich gemacht, da nach Abschluss des ersten Verfahrens das noch schwebende zweite Verfahren jedem Gnadenakt entgegenstehen würde."*[5]

The central legal protection department of the AA was of the opinion that this law had changed nothing. The problem of war criminals had not been solved. The reparations questions were still open. Merten's defence lawyer expressed the opinion that *"es berechtigt ist zu sagen, dass dieses Gesetz praktisch überhaupt keinen Fortschritt bringt, im Gegenteil es verhindert die Erledigung eines Teiles der Fälle durch Ablauf der Verjährung."*[6]

The first Trial

By 21 February 1959 Merten had spent 21 month in solitary confinement in the Averof prison in Athens. On this date the trial began at a special military court. The chairman of the tribunal was colonel Ioannis Kokoretsas. The minister of justice, K. Tsatsos, had instructed him to push the case through in two weeks and to reject all private plaintiffs. The first instruction failed because the proceedings lasted until 5 March. Kokoretsas complied with the second instruction already on the first day of the trial when he rejected all private suits. The real reason for the rejection may be found in the field of politics. Among lawyers who represented

1 Spiliotis, *op. cit.*, p. 121f.
2 Übersetzung Gesetz No. 3933: BA B 141/9573, p. 168.
3 Botschaft an AA am 16. Januar 1959: BA B 141/9573, pp. 169f, 172f.
4 BA B 141/9573, p. 174.
5 Aide Mémoire: BA B 141/9573, p. 176.
6 Walter an Zenrtale Rechtsschutzstelle am 5. Februar 1959: BA B 141/9573, p. 174f.

Jewish interests was the well known leftist Ilias Tsirimokos of the EDA. Obviously the government wanted to avoid a conflagration in court.[1]

Tousis main aim was the enforcement of the reparations claim. Apparently he was not informed that the 200 million DM investment credit was a tarnished reparation. In order to avoid a release of Merten at the end of the first trial Tousis had seen to it that there would be a second trial. The Greek Government had intended that the trial would go off without a hitch but in the days before the trial began there had been a demagogic press campaign against Merten which heated the atmosphere. When Merten in handcuffs was led up the outside staircase aggressive shouts were heard from a big crowd. The courtroom was packed full. Journalists from Greece and foreign countries observed the trial. Among the observers was the lawyer Dieter Posser of the law office of Gustav Heinemann in Essen.[2]

There were 100 witnesses of the prosecution and 50 of the defence. The trial had three phases. During the first, from 11 to 18 February, the witnesses of the prosecution were heard. On 19 and 20 February the Greek defence witnesses were heard and from 20 to 25 February the foreign witnesses. Afterwards Merten was heard. On 5 March the judgement was pronounced: 25 years imprisonment, five years more than the state attorney had demanded.

There had been three topics which were dealt with. (1) The activities which led to the events on 11 July 1942 on the *Plateia Eleftherias* and to the disappropriation of the Jewish cemetery of Thessaloniki. (2) The transport of the Jews of Salonika to the extermination camps in Poland. (3) The shooting of the hostages and the plundering of the shops in Salonika. Since it is impossible to deal with each testimony we will take a closer look at the topics mentioned earlier.

The events of 11 July 1942 and the disappropriation of the Jewish cemetery

Before the war there had been a prosperous Jewish community of 60,000 souls in Thessaloniki. Their ancestors had fled from the persecution of the Spanish inquisition to the Ottoman Empire in late 15th century. Most of them still spoke a mixed language out of old Castilian and Jewish and lived in their own world separated from the Greek environment.[3]

In June 1941 the commando Rosenberg had appeared and had confiscated the huge library and art treasures of the Jewish community and had plundered the synagogues. The famine of the winter 1941 had hit the poorer Jews more heavily than their Greek fellow citizens who still had relatives in the country side. Until summer 1942 the Germans left the Jews alone. But then local authorities of the Wehrmacht began with a building measure i.e the building of roads and repair of railway lines. According to Hague Convention such works had to be made by the Greek administration of Macedonia. However the Governor General of Macedonia, former General Athanasios Chrysochoou declared that he did not have the necessary financial means to pay the workers. Instead he proposed to conscript several thousand Jews of certain age groups to do this job.[4] The building measure already mentioned was induced by the Army Group, the executing officer was the administrative officer (Kriegsverwaltungsrat) Dr. Karl Marbach whose rank was that of a captain.

---

1 Spiliotis, *op. cit.*, p. 131f.

2 *Ibidem.*

3 Esther Benbassa, *Die Geschichte der Sephardischen Juden. Von Toledo bis Saloniki* (Bochum: Winkler, 2005).

4 Hagen Fleischer, *Im Kreuzschatten der Mächte. Griechenland 1941-1944* (Frankfurt, Bern, New York: Peter Lang, 1986), p. 365. According to the Hague Convention the building of roads by citizens able to work of an occupied country was allowed. Zentrale Stelle Ludwigsburg (ZstL) 508 AR-Z139/59, Einstellungsverfügung der Staatsanwaltschaft Berlin vom 4.Juni 1968, Prozessgeschichte, p. 349.

On 9, 10 and 11 July 1942 the Nazi newspaper *Nea Evropi,* which appeared in Thessaloniki, demanded in the name of the Greek Governor General that all Jews of the military classes of the years 1897 to 1924 should come to the *Plateia Eleftherias* on 11 July 1942 to be registered.[1] There happened excesses and assaults from the German side.[2] The registration lasted two day but the mistreatments were allegedly stopped on the second day by superiors.[3]

There were witnesses in court who stated that Merten had been there. Merten, however, was verifiably in Germany on 11 July 1942. It was the 3 August 1942 when he was ordered to travel from Marburg to Thessaloniki where he arrived on 10 August 1942.[4] The Berlin prosecution office stated in 1968: *"Die Zeugen, die Dr. Merten schon am 11. Juli 1942 auf dem Freiheitsplatz in Saloniki gesehen haben wollen, müssen sich irren. Möglicherweise bringen sie verschiedene Personen und Ereignisse durcheinander. Dazu könnte beigetragen haben, dass sie für die politischen und rassischen Verfolgungen, denen sie von Seiten der deutschen Besatzung ausgesetzt waren, ganz allgemein den scheinbar allmächtigen Leiter der Militärverwaltung Dr. Merten verantwortlich gemacht haben."* The special military court saw this also and exonerated Merten from this point.[5]

The 2,000 conscripts were used to build roads and work in quarries. Most of them were physically not fit for these activities. Besides this they were fed badly and accommodated miserably: *"Zum größten Teil mussten die Juden unter freiem Himmel schlafen."* Many became ill and quite a number died. According to Molho sometimes 60 percent were ill. The mortality rose to 12 percent. The treatment by the German organization Todt was allegedly brutal .[6]

The German authorities recognized that the Jewish forced labour was of little use and suggested to engage Greek road builders. But these would work only if the were paid accordingly. The new Kriegsverwaltungsrat, Dr. Max Merten, who had begun his work in August 1942 contacted the leadership of the Jewish community on 13 October 1942 and suggested that they should pay 3,5 milliards Drachmae transfer fee and the forced labour would end. The Jewish community managed to collect 2 milliards Drachmae (about 10,000 golden pounds Sterling).[7] After renewed negotiations it was agreed that the remaining sum would covered by the transfer of the Jewish cemetery to the city of Thessaloniki which had since long wanted the cemetery and it would pay the rest sum. It is improbable that the newcomer Merten developed the idea with the cemetery. It can be assumed that the proposal came from the interested Greek side.[8]

---

1 ZStL 508 AR-Z139/59 Prozessgeschichte, p. 216.

2 Michael Molho, *In Memoriam. Hommage aux Victimes Juives des Nazis en Grèce* (Salonique, 1948), p. 43; "Griechenland: Ihr Onkel Konstantin. Kriegsverbrechen" *Der Spiegel* 40 (28. September 1960), p 30f. *"Während einer nach dem anderen registriert und mit einem Arbeitsausweis versehen wurde, vertrieb sich der divisionsstarke Rest die Zeit mit gymnastischen Übungen. Die Wachen feuerten sie mit Peitschenschlägen an. Wer auf dem schattenlosen Freiheitsplatz ohnmächtig wurde, bekam Wasser über den Kopf. Die Registrierten durften sich entfernen - die ersten hundert Meter wahlweise auf dem Bauch robbend oder Purzelbäume schlagend."*

3 ZStL 508 AR-Z139/59 Prozessgeschichte, p. 222.

4 *Ibidem*, p. 228f.

5 *Ibidem*, p. 230.

6 Molho, *op. cit.*, pp. 44f, 47; ZStL 508 AR-Z139/59 Prozessgeschichte, p.223-228.

7 According to data of Neubacher in Oktober 1942 the price of ome golden pound was 300.000 Drachmae thus it would have been 6,666 golden pounds. Hermann Neubacher, *Sonderauftrag Südost 1940-1945. Bericht eines fliegenden Diplomaten* (Seeheim: Buchkreis, 1966), p. 74.

8 Molho, *op. cit.*, p. 56. *"Depuis longtemps, certains protagonistes de la politique de clocher, férus d'un urbanisme d'occasion, voulaient obtenir la désaffectation du cimetière juif. Profitant de la présence des Nazis dans le pays, quelques uns d'entre eux, oublieux de toute pudeur et de toute délicatesse morale et patriotique, s'appuyèrent honteusement sur l'envahisseur, pour détruire précipitamment la vielle nécropole qui avait une valeur archéolo-*

The Jewish community managed to collect the money and the surviving forced labourers were set free. The cemetery was transferred into the property of Thessaloniki. In December 1942 the graves were flattened and the grave stones destroyed or used as building material. Whether the town of Thessaloniki paid the transfer sum is unknown but probable that the cemetery became property of the town of Thessaloniki and not, as one often reads, property of the Wehrmacht. In the latter case it would have been returned to the Jewish community after the end of the war. Today the university of Thessaloniki is on this compound.[1]

Merten used the money as agreed to hire Greek workers.[2] In the order to dismiss the case of the Berlin prosecution office one reads that *"die Nötigung der jüdischen Gemeinde Salonikis zur Zahlung eines Lösegeldes für die völkerrechtswidrig zur Zwangsarbeit eingesetzten Juden rechtswidrig war."* But Merten wanted to help the Jews and had to decide between two evils. He could only *"seine höherrangige Pflicht erfüllen können, die Juden aus ihrer lebensbedrohlichen Zwangslage zu befreien."*[3]

The transfer of the Jews

Half a year later, on 6 February 1943 the next "round" of the final solution began when SS-Hauptsturmführer Dieter Wisliceny and Alois Brunner arrived in Thessaloniki on orders of the Reichssicherheitshauptamtes. Wisliceny carried preformulated orders for the preparation of the Endlösung with him which had been applied in other countries before. On the same day Merten signed in the name of the Befehlshaber Saloniki-Ägäis the first such order which forced all Greek Jews to wear a yellow star and to live in a ghetto. Their shops should also be marked. The execution of this order would be controlled by an SD-commando.[4] During the Athenian trial the former Obermilitärverwaltungsrat of army group E, Theodor Parisius, who had belonged to the same office as Merten, stated that Merten signed with the knowledge of the commander.[5]

On 8 February 1943 Wisliceny called the chief rabbi Zvi Koretz. Koretz was born in 1884 in Rzeszów in Galicia. After studies in Berlin he became a rabbi. I 1933 the Jewish community of Thessaloniki elected him as a rabbi and in 1938 as chief rabbi. At the end of 1942 he was made president of the community. It had been him with whom Merten negotiated the deal about the cemetery. The community believed that because of his knowledge of German Koretz would achieve the best for them. As he knew the Germans he was convinced that one could achieve the best by unconditional obedience and therefore he demanded from his community to obey the German orders. Thus he became a submissive tool of Wisliceny and Brunner.

On 12 February Wisliceny ordered the application of the Nuremberg laws. After the establishment of the ghetto *Baron Hirsch,* Jewish regulators and policemen appointed and other measures were taken to socially isolate the Jews. In March the Jewish fortunes were confiscated. On 15 March the first and in May the last transport left Salonika. Til autumn 1943

---

gique, historique, traditionnelle, sentimentale et artistique." Dazu auch AG Tiergarten 353 AR 1680/61, Anlage 1.

1 Molho, *op. cit.*, pp. 48f, 56. The often heard claim that the Wehrmacht had intended to erect an ammunition depot is in view of the position of the cemetery absurd.

2 ZStL 508 AR-Z139/59 Prozessgeschichte, p. 343.

3 *Ibidem*, pp. 354, 359..

4 Facsimile des Befehls in Molho, *op. cit.*, p. 135. To these orders Merten ZStL 508 AR-Z139/59 Prozessgeschichte, p. 134f; AG Tiergarten 353 AR 1680/61, p, 14.

5 Botschaft an AA 503-88 No. 319/59 vom 26. Februar 1959, p. 2: AA Referat 206 Band Nr. 134.

46,091 Jews were transferred, most of them to Auschwitz-Birkenau. 95 percent of the Jewish population of Thessaloniki was killed.[1]

Already at that time Koretz was attacked because of his cooperation with the SD (Sicherheitsdienst - Security Service) and he was accused to not to have had enough courage. He had done nothing to save his community from the deportation and had blindly obeyed the orders of the SD. He had not understood anything and anticipated nothing. On 17 March when the transports to Poland had already begun he said in a synagogue in Salonika that all Jews would be transported to Poland where they could begin a new life among their fellow Jews. Koretz appealed to the rich to show solidarity with the poors because there had been rumours that only the poors would be deported. He left the synagogue under boos protected by the Jewish police.[2] Koretz himself was deported in August 1943 together with his family and 74 members of the community and 367 Jews who had Spanish passports to Bergen Belsen as special detainees. He survived the war and died shortly after its end.

Since the orders were signed alternately by Merten and Wisliceny the concerned persons and the Greek public gained the impression that Merten was responsible for the deportation of the Jews. It was not understood who was the initiator of the commands and that Merten was only an executive organ. In Saloniki the Wehrmacht in the person of the Befehlshaber Saloniki-Ägäis (til 31 December 1942 General Curt von Krenzki, then for two weeks General Bogislav von Studnitz and since 20 January 1943 General Johannes Haarde) cooperated with the SS but the commanders were cautious enough not to expose themselves and let the lowest rank, Merten, do the dirty work. In the beginning Merten signed the first two orders: *"Für den Befehlshaber Saloniki-Ägäis. Der Chef des Stabes. Dr. Merten. Kriegsverwaltungsrat."* But from the third order on he signed by putting a "I. A. (In Auftrag - on behalf) in front of his signature. This was the cautious attempt to distance himself from the sinister events. Wisliceny on the other hand signed with his name and "SS-Hauptsturmführer".[3]

Spiliotis interpreted Merten's i. A. as a proof for Merten's active participation in the deportation of the Jews. In order to prove this she quotes a statement by Eichmann during his trial in Israel: *"Wenn Dr. Merten als Vertreter des Militärbefehlshabers gegen die Deportation protestiert hätte, hätte Brunner die Deportation nicht durchführen können, denn das Primat in allen diesen Fragen und die Befehlsgewalt lag bei Dr. Merten als Vertreter des Militärbefehlshabers. Es ist insofern richtig, ... weil [...] diese selbe Sache sich in allen Ländern gleichermaßen in Anwendung bringen läßt, ... wo Militärbefehlshaber waren, ... Hätte ein Militärbefehlshaber dagegen sein Veto eingelegt, [...] hätte auch ein Befehl des Reichsführers [Himmler...] dann in diesem Gebiet nicht durchgeführt werden können."*[4] Eichmann's statement is simply wrong. It was one his attempt to justify his behaviour to whitewash himself. Had Merten dared to refuse a signature he would have come into the greatest trouble. Additionally Eichmann knew that Merten had incriminated him in his statements in Athens. Thus it was simply revenge.

It is known that Merten constantly tried to save Jews as long as it did not endanger himself. The Red Cross delegate, the Swiss Rene Burckhardt, confirmed that Merten did as much as possible to protect the Jews of Saloniki. When he learned that the SD commando would arrive soon he informed Burckhardt. The latter warned the chief rabbi Koretz who however

1 *Ibidem*, pp. 59-84.

2 *Ibidem*, p. 84.

3 Facsimiles *ibidem*, pp. 135-145. During his interrogation in Bratislava on 27 June 1947 Wisliceny alleged, that he had not signed one order. The prosecution Berlin stated that Wisliceny tried to present Brunner and Merten as the main culprits, ZStL 508 AR-Z139/59 Prozessgeschichte, p. 131.

4 Spiliotis, *op. cit.*, p. 63.

did not react. But Burckhardt managed to induce some Jewish youths to flee.[1] When the SD commando arrived Merten told Burckhardt that from now on he could do nothing any more.[2] On 28 December 1946 Burckhardt wrote in his finale report about his activities in Salonika to the then president of the International Red Cross Carl Burckhardt that Merten had given valuable help to the Red Cross. Contrary to the will of Wisliceny he had delivered food to the Jews in the ghetto. *"Zusammenfassend glaube ich persönlich, dass Dr. Max Merten von Seiten der Alliierten für seine Tätigkeit in Saloniki [...] eine Sonderbehandlung verdient, besonders was seine versteckte Hilfe an die Israeliten und seine korrekte Behandlung anbetraf."*[3]

Burckhardt watched the deportation of the Jews and developed an idea how women and children could be saved by bringing them to another country. On 29 May 1961 Merten testified the following in his hearing in the Eichmann trial: *"Jeden Monat kamen ein oder zwei Dampfer des Roten Kreuzes nach Saloniki, die leer nach Canada zurückfuhren. Dr. Burkhardt wollte Frauen und Kinder mit diesen Dampfern herausbringen. Zufälligerweise kamen im März 1943 zwei Dampfer gleichzeitig an, so dass die Möglichkeit bestanden hätte, eine Zahl von zehntausend Personen bei dieser oder der nächsten Fahrt mitzunehmen."*[4]

Because in December 1942 the Swiss Consulate in Salonika had been closed Bruckhardt contacted Merten.[5] The two agreed that Burckhardt would send a telegram to Merten. Merten would send this telegram via Dr. Günther Altenburg (Bevollmächtigter des Reiches in Griechenland) to the German Red Cross in Berlin asking to pass it on to the ICRC (International Committee of the Red Cross) in Geneva. As Merten distrusted Altenburg, because he closely cooperated with the SD, on 13 March he additionally sent the telegram directly to the Red Cross in Berlin.[6]

The text of the telegram read: *"Bitten Interrotkreuz Metropole Genf drahten ANFANG Deportation fünfundvierzig Tausend Juden Saloniki fast bestimmt STOP Dringliche Prüfung mit betreffenden Regierungen Deportation Frauen und Kinder Palestina erforderlich."*[7] On 17 March Altenburg contacted the representative of the ICRC in Athens, the Swiss Jean d'Amman, and made clear to him that the deportation of the Jews was a purely political matter which was no concern for the ICRC. Burckhardt had transgressed his competence and had mingled in purely German affairs. Burckhardt must leave Greece but this should be done in a discreet way. D'Amman called Burkhardt and informed him. Burckhardt agreed but he would leave only when an adequate substitute had arrived. This, however, took three months.[8] But without Merten's help the telegram would never have arrived in Geneva.

In his testimony in the Eichmann case Merten stated that he had spoken with Eichman about the departure of the women and children, at first via telephone from Salonika and then directly in Berlin and Eichmann had accepted his proposals. However in Berlin Globke objected. After his return to Salonika he tried twice to get in contact with the British. The second effort succeeded but the British side refused to accept the transport. Therefore the

1 Burkhardt an Staatsanwalt Bauer am 31. Januar 1961: Archiv für Christlich Demokratische Politik I-070-082/2.
2 AA Referat 206 Band 135: 8 JS 78/61 p. 74.
3 Carl Burckhardt an Fredicia am 9. Mai 1961: Archiv für Christlich Demokratische Politik I-070-100/2 c.
4 Aussage Merten: AG Tiergarten 353 AR 1680/61, p. 16. The existence of ths plan is verified by the Merci-diary. http://www.gemeinde.bozen.it/UploadDocs/6755_Merci_deutsch.pdf, p. 55.
5 Steven Bowman, "Another Righteous Gentile: The IRRC Representative in Salonika" *Thetis* 3 (1996), p. 219.
6 Aussage Merten: AG Tiergarten 353 AR 1680/61, p. 16.
7 Text in AG Tiergarten 353 AR 1680/61 Anlage 9 und Jean-Claude Favez, *Une mission impossible? Le CICR, les déportations et les camps de concentrations nazi* (Lausanne, 1988), p. 254.
8 Bowman, *op. cit.*, p. 219.

relief operation could not take place.[1] Unfortunately there is no source from a third party confirming this story.

During the Athens trial the former Italian consul, Guiseppe Castrucci, gave testimony in favour of Merten. He, the consul, had tried to save the Jews from the grip of the SS by bringing them to Athens in the Italian occupation zone. For this purpose he had issued Italian passports to Jews. In July 1943 an Italian military train had gone from Salonika to Athens with more than 300 Jews. *"Ohne Unterstützung von Merten wäre diese Rettung der Juden nicht möglich gewesen, denn Merten habe den Zug mit den Juden fahren lassen, obgleich er gewusst habe, dass ihnen die italienischen Pässe nicht zustanden und die Gestapo dadurch getäuscht wurde."* An affidavit of the Jewish community conformed this in 1946.[2] During the first months of the deportations it was the Italian General Consul Guelfo Zamboni who freed "Italians" out of the Baron von Hirsch ghetto.[3] Merten's lawyer, Matsoukas, stated in his final defence speech that in the first bill of indictment Merten had not been accused of having participated in the deportation of the Jews.[4] Wolfgang Breyer published more cases in his dissertation how Merten helped Greeks and Greek Jews.[5]

Attached to Merten's office was a big office of translators in which many graduates of the German school of Salonika worked. In 2000 Breyer succeeded in contacting one of them, a certain Juli B. Pierbonis. She spoke very positively about Merten and told that he had had a gifted young man as right hand who was an Austrian Jew; Unfortunately he died a year later of eye tuberculosis. Another graduate of the German school and later wife of the Heidelberg university professor of archaeology Jörg Schäfer, who also had worked in Merten's office, also spoke very positively about Merten. She remembered the name of Merten's right hand: Alexander Asseo. Pierbonis told that Asseo's mother stemmed of the famous Austrian musician family of Gelber. After the Germens occupied Greece the Asseo family changed its name into Astos which sound less suspicious. Merten allegedly saved the famous Greek actor Manos Katrakis from death by starvation.[6] Katrakis later joined EAM/ELAS and during the civil war he was interned in Makronissos.

Shooting of Hostages and Executions

Another point of the indictment against Merten were reprisals against the civil population. The central legal protection department of the AA (ZRS) made an effort to clear up the command structures. From August 1942 to the end of the year there had been a Wehrmachtsbefehlshaber Südost (Alexander Löhr) based in Thessaloniki. In January 1943 this was changed into OB (Oberbefehlshaber) Südost and Army Group E. Under his orders were the Befehlshaber Saloniki-Ägäis (since 20 January 1943 Johannes Haarde) and the Befehlshaber Südgriechenland (Wilhelm Speidel). Both were responsible for the administration of occupied

1 Aussage Merten: AG Tiergarten 353 AR 1680/61, pp. 16-19. *Der Spiegel* wrote in 1960, that Lord Moyne who was responsible for British mandated territory Palestine had refused to let enter such a great number of Jews the country. "Kriegsverbrechen Griechenland. Ihr Onkel Konstantin" *Der Spiegel* 40 (28. September 1960), p. 32.

2 Botschaft an AA 503-88 No. 319/59 vom 26. Februar 1959, p. 4: AA Referat 206 Band Nr. 134; Merci wrote a diary: http://www.gemeinde.bozen.it/UploadDocs/6755_Merci_deutsch.pdf. According to the diary Merten saved 436 persons. Merci wrote further that Merten (p. 46), signed the permits of the Jews so the could pass unhindered.

3 Tagebuch Merci p. 40.

4 Botschaft an AA 503-88 No. 319/59 vom 26. Februar 1959, p. 2: AA Referat 206 Band Nr. 134.

5 Breyer, *op. cit.*, pp. 117-120.

6 *Ibidem*, p. 55.

Greece. The office of the Befehlshaber Saloniki-Ägäis had the rank of an upper field command (Oberfeldkommandatur). Merten was under its command.[1]

The ZRS asked the former chief of staff of the army group E and Speidel to contribute their knowledge to the case. Speidel who had been sentenced to jail by the 6th Nuremberg trial replied sarcastically that he "an experienced war criminal" was ready to make Merten's fate easier. He wrote a paper on the military assignments but refused that this paper would be presented in Athens. He wondered why these stories would be warmed up again.[2]

In the Athens trial the former administrative officer Parisius stated that *"ein Kriegsverwaltungsrat keinerlei Exekutivbefugnisse oder Weisungsrechte an Einheiten der Wehrmacht oder Polizei gehabt habe. [...] Zu der Frage der Geiselerschießungen legte Parisius unter Hervorhebung der begrenzten Befugnisse der Militärverwaltung eingehend dar, dass Merten seiner ganzen Zuständigkeit nach hiermit nichts zu tun gehabt habe."* The former lt. General Gerhard Engel supported this and then wrote about the "relocation" of the Jews. On 2 November 1941 Hitler gave Himmler a special authority *"die Umsiedlung mit einem SS-Sonderkommando durchzuführen, dabei aber ausdrücklich befohlen, dass der Militärbefehlshaber Saloniki nur soweit dringend erforderlich einzuschalten sei."* He was to be informed but at the same time be told *"diese Maßnahmen unter keinen Umständen zu stören."*[3]

The prosecution had accused Merten of having participated in the shooting of 680 Greek hostages or to have ordered them. The testimonies of Parisius and Engel, both former officers, impressed the military judges so much that they discharged Merten in this case. Especially Engel impressed the Greek military: *"Als Engel auf Befragen erklärte, er habe bei der Infanterie gedient, sagte einer der militärischen Beisitzer lächelnd auf Deutsch: 'Wir sind Kameraden'."*[4]

In another case the court accused Merten that he had allegedly ordered the shooting of five Jews among them two children and sentenced to 18 years prison [5] The prosecution of Berlin which also examined the case doubted that Merten had the competence to order the shooting and stated that two adults (Benveniste and Kamhi) were shot on the order of an unknown person. Regarding the children they found out that there was an error of names, they were not related to the adults. The Berlin prosecution could not find any guilt with Merten.[6]

The Confiscation of Jewish Fortunes

Like in Germany the fortunes of the Jews were confiscated in Greece also. On 20 February 1943 the Jews were forbidden to sell their fortunes. From the same day on troops of Greek citizens under the lead of SD special commandos and of the an agent with the name Laskaris Papanaoum were on their way to confiscate all Jewish shops and seal them.[7] On 7 March an order was released by Merten (MV pol 5 2839 Dr. Me) which stemmed from Wisliceny which demanded that trustees should be appointed for all Jewish shops and handicraft enterprises. For their supervision an office for the administration of the Jewish fortunes (*Υπηρεσία Διαχειρίσεως Ισραηλιτικών Περιουσιών*, YDIP) would be established. The Governor General of Macedonia controlled this real estate office of Thessaloniki. In the middle of March Wisliceny informed the YDIP that the Jewish fortunes would be transferred to the Greek state. On 20

1 Richter, *Revolution*, p. 193.
2 Spiliotis, *op. cit.*, p. 97. She caracterized Speidel's remark as cynical.
3 Botschaft an AA 503-88 No. 319/59 vom 26. Februar 1959, p. 1: AA Referat 206 Band Nr. 134.
4 Botschaft an AA 503-88 No. 381/1959 Anlage vom 6. März 1959; AA Referat 206 Band Nr. 135.
5 Ibidem.
6 ZStL 508 AR-Z139/59 Prozessgeschichte, pp. 203-215.
7 *Ibidem*, p. 241f.

May Merten published the according order. It read: The existing Jewish property in the realm of the Militärkommandantur Saloniki-Ägäis would be transferred to the Greek state. The trustees which were appointed by the Governor General could freely dispose of it. The shops should continue. Under German control 300 trustees were appointed.[1]

Breyer described in his thesis a great number of cases where Jewish enterprises were transferred to private citizens. There were cases where relatives or acquaintances of Greek collaborators, e.g. Papanaoum were the beneficiaries. Informers were also entitled to Jewish fortunes. The Governor General distributed the empty Jewish apartments [2] It can be assumed that great parts of the Jewish property was "hellenized" and remained so similarly as in post-war Germany the arianized property.

On 13 March Merten released an order which on 15 March was supplemented by one of Wisliceny by which the Jews of Thessaloniki ware requested to transact their liquid funds and their articles of value by the Jewish community, i.e. the occupation forces; in case of rejections punishment threatened.[3] Allegedly 280 milliard Drachmae were collected. This sounds impressive but in view of the galloping inflation then it was not more than the sum which was paid for the relief of the forced labourers. After the war Wisliceny claimed before the IMT (International Military Tribunal) that the collected money was taken over by the military administration. Merten said that the collected jewelry was sent to the Embassy in Athens and from there by air transport to Germany. The latter coincides with an order by Goering of 5 November 1941 which ruled that all precious metal and jewelry should be delivered to the central pay office of the Reich.[4] It cannot be assumed that greater parts "diffused".

Two weeks after the return of the government in exile of Papandreou in October 1944 it decided to return the Jewish assets but it did not work. When in summer 1945 the first survivors of the camps returned they found the trustees of the occupation regime in their houses. Besides that many homeless people had occupied the empty houses something which became stronger during the civil war. The improved restitution law of 1945 was ratified only in 1949 after the end of the civil war and only under the pressure of he US and the World Jewish Congress.[5]

After the war the son of a jew who had been killed in Auschwitz wanted the shop of his father back from the trustee. When he refused the restitution the son had to go to court. The court decided that the son should submit the certificate of death of his father from Auschwitz. As this was impossible the trustee could keep the shop. If a shop was returned then it was empty. Heirs had great difficulties getting back their heritage. Of course there were correct retrotransfers but these were not the rule. Therefore in Greece also there were beneficiaries of the holocaust.[6]

The Treasures of Merten

Because Merten was involved in the handling of the confiscated Jewish properties the Greek side insinuated that he had enriched himself had and had collected treasures. Allegedly he brought a small part to his wife who lived in Hungary then, a greater part he hid somewhere

---

1 *Ibidem*, pp. 242-248.

2 So Breyer, *op. cit.*, pp. 75-85. Also Stratos Dordanas and Vaios Kalogrias, "Die jüdische Gemeinde von Thessaloniki während der deutschen Besatzungszeit 1941-1944: Zwischengemeindliche Beziehungen, Ghettoisierung und Deportation" *PaRDeS Zeitschrift der Vereinigung für Jüdische Studien* 17 (Potsdam, 2011), p. 114.

3 ZStL 508 AR-Z139/59 Prozessgeschichte, p. 299.

4 *Ibidem*, p. 302.

5 Hagen Fleischer, "Saloniki unter dem Hakenkreuz" Vortrag (Thessaloniki, 15. März 2011).

6 Mitteilungen von Samuel Hassid in mehreren E-Mails an den Verfasser im Juli 2012.

in Greece. This rumour circulated in Greece for decades as I personally remember but nobody took it seriously.

But in 1999 the rumour assumed a new quality when a certain Konstantinos Vrettos contacted the Jewish community in Thessaloniki via his lawyer. He claimed that he knew where the treasures were which Merten had stolen from the Jews. He been a cell mate of Merten in the Averof jail. (Merten ahd been in cellular confinement all the time). Merten had allegedly told him that his treasure consisted out of 46 crates with 230,000 golden pounds, one box with 300 huge diamonds and a Holy Chalice (!). He had brought his treasure with a submarine of the German navy to the Mycenaean gulf, loaded it on a kaiki with the help of three German officers and sunk it at a certain point into the sea. Then he allegedly shot the three officers to keep his secret and returned to Thessaloniki. Vrettos enriched the story by mentioning people who had never existed. Vrettos declared himself ready to tell the Jewish community the place where the treasure was - contingent upon a payment of 200,000 Euros. It is unknown whether this sum was paid. Fact is however that in summer 2000 civil servants, private people and members of the Jewish community dived for the treasures. The TV was transmitting live. Of course nothing was found. In 2002 it became known that Vrettos was a criminal who had been in jail several times.[1]

Until now this tale could be considered as a grotesque story à la Indiana Jones over which one could be amused. But on 12 August 2000 MDR (Mitteldeutscher Rundfunk) reported in the news series *Brisant* about the diving action. In the sea in front of Kalamata a gold treasure was searched, *"bestehend aus Goldbarren, Goldmünzen und Juwelen im heutigen Wert von 40 bis 45 Mrd. DM (!), der hier 1944 versenkt worden sein soll. Diese Schätze sollen während der deutschen Besatzungszeit den Juden von Thessaloniki abgenommen worden sein mit dem Versprechen, dass sie dafür nicht deportiert werden würden. Initiator dieser Sache sei der deutsche Offizier Dr. Max Merten gewesen, und er habe die betreffende Information einem nahen Vertrauten gegeben. Auch das ZDF übernahm diesen Beitrag am 18. August in seinem 'Heute-Journal'."*[2] It is difficult to state what is more astonishing the incompetence of the responsible editorial journalists or their total ignorance of Greek affairs.

The Judgement

The military prosecutor had demanded a total punishment of 140 years jail for all individual cases which was reduced to a realistic 20 years jail sentence. The verdict of 5 March 1959 came to a total of 125 years which were concentrated and reduced to 25 years prison and confiscation of Merten's proporties.[3] The German Embassy sent a report on the reactions of the Greek public in Athens: *"Das Urteil hat hier große Überraschung ausgelöst. Besonders in Kreisen der griechischen Juristen war man zum Teil sogar empört. Allgemein hatte man damit gerechnet, dass ein Urteil ergehen würde, das zwischen Freispruch und höchstens acht Jahren Freiheitsstrafe liegen würde. Insbesondere lässt sich das Urteil mit dem Ergebnis der Beweisaufnahme und der ganzen Durchführung des Verfahrens einfach nicht in Einklang bringen."* An explanation was not expected even when the text of the judgement was submitted in writing. In the Greek military judiciary explanatory statements do not exist nor lines of argument. The judgement consisted only of a statement of the penalty.[4]

---

1 *Βημαγαζίνο* (12. September 2004), pp. 68-73.
2 Breyer, *op. cit.*, p. 81.
3 Botschaft an AA 503-88 No. 381/1959 Anlage vom 6. März 1959; AA Referat 206 Band Nr. 135; Breyer, *op. cit.*, pp. 120-123.
4 Botschaft an AA 503-88 No. 381/1959 vom 6. März 1959; AA Referat 206 Band Nr. 135.

This kind of conduct of a case reminds one of the trials against the left after the Dekemvriana when only incriminating arguments and no exonerating ones were noted. From the beginning of the trial the judgement was fixed.

Lawyer Posser who had observed the trial, informed Heinemann about the judgement. Both considered it a total judicial wrongdoing. In their eyes the judgement was a crass contradiction of the facts. In a letter to the budget committee MP Heinemann demanded that the financial agreement should be set back.[1] Obviously Heinemann had recognized the connection between the Merten case and the payment of tarnished reparations.

However Merten did not only get into the twilight of the final solution. As he was the "interface" between the Wehrmacht and the Greek administration and the population he was responsible for the provisioning. He was the person who was noticed by the Greek population no wonder that they called him the "archont" or king of Salonika. Because the accusations of corruption are based on hearsay they must be taken seriously. If one has not met Merten personally it is difficult to state whether he was honest and overstrained or a enigmatic character as it is often heard. It can not be excluded that the Greeks simply projected the behaviour of Greek bureaucrats onto Merten. Merten was not the war criminal as he is described to this day.

However one can understand Samuel Hassid when he writes: *"Although our notion of his powers may be exaggerated, Merten cannot be considered innocent in the eyes of most of us Greek Jews. He might not have participated in the most heinous of Holocaust crimes, but he was directly involved in the destruction of our community. More distressing, however, than the case per se is the feeling that justice was not served in the case of Greece and its citizens (Jews, but also Christians ...) - which makes the Merten case a symbol. If one accepts his defence that he was not responsible for most of the crimes attributed to him, one must simultaneously acknowledge the fact that almost none of those allegedly responsible were punished either..."*[2]

Later he wrote: *"I am sure we all agree though that something is wrong somewhere: for the murder of the appr. 70,000 Jews in Greece, nobody paid any price!!!"*[3] Unfortunately this statement of Hassid is right. Alois Brunner was able to go into hiding in Germany until 1954 and when arrest threatened he fled to Syria where he probably died some years ago. Wisliceny continued his horrible work until the end of the war. His last victims were the Hungarian Jews. In the Nuremberg Trial he was a witness for the prosecution. His statements were even used in the Eichmann trial in Jerusalem in 1961. After the end of the Nuremberg Trial he was extradited to the ĈSSR where in 1948 he was put to trial, sentenced to death and executed in February 1948. Eichmann's fate is known. Two of the main culprits did not escape punishment though not by Greek courts.

A GDR Intermezzo

During the whole Marten affair the GDR (East Germany) had supplied incriminating evidence against Merten and the Federal Republic.[4] In March 1959 a group of leftist and liberal deputies travelled to the GDR. Allegedly Ulbricht offered reparation payments if Greece

1 ZRS-Aufzeichnung über Unterredung mit Heinemann und Posser mit AA- und ZRS-Vertretern am 8. April 1959 vom 10. April 1959: AA Referat 206 Band Nr. 134; Spiliotis, *op. cit.*, p. 134.

2 Samuel Hassid, *The Trial of Max Merten in the Changing Mirrors of Time and Place* (Technion Haifa, 2002).

3 http://www.yvelia.com/kolhakehila/board/jews_greece_wwii/jews_greece_wwii.html.

4 Andreas Stergiou, *Im Spagat zwischen Solidarität und Realpolitik. Die Beziehungen zwischen der DDR und Griechenland und das Verhältnis der SED zur KKE* (Möhnesee: Bibliopolis, 2001), p. 99.

recognized the GDR. West-Germany would only pay compensations to victims of racial and religious persecution.[1] If this offer was initiated by Ulbricht is not known. But it is clear that such an offer would never be accepted by the right wing ERE Government. Thus the East German Government could make this offer without any risk because it would be rejected.. It was a propaganda manoeuvre which should diminish the reputation of West Germany and strengthen the EDA in their fight against the Greek Government. Besides that the recipients of the DDR reparation payments would have been only former EAM/ELAS members i.e. leftists.

But the GDR offensive was not confined to transferring incriminating material against Merten to the EDA because EDA asked for material against Karamanlis, Makris and the future "neutral" member of the Cypriot High Court, Ernst Forsthoff which might be used against them.[2] In November 1959 the EDA deputy Komninos Pyromaglou, appeared in east-Berlin to obtain material against Merten. He promised the send a list with 300 war criminals to the GDR so that they could search for incriminating material.[3] Such contacts continued in 1960 as is proved by the GDR visit of the deputy Michail Kyrkos.[4]

Merten's Attempt for Revenge

As was already stated on 18 February 1959 the law on suspension of the persecution of war crimes entered into force. However the word amnesty did not exist in the text of the law. On 25 March Merten had been condemned to 25years of prison. Though the Greek Government had promised transfer him to Germany soon after the proclamation of the sentence, in May 1959 Merten was still in the prison though Ambassador Seelos had spoken several times about this with Karamanlis. Ambassador Ypsilantis hinted that they were waiting for a suitable moment when this release could be organized without greater excitement of the public.[5]

Probably they kept Merten in prison to be abler to exert pressure during the now beginning negotiations on reparations of Nazi crimes.[6] When the negotiations had successfully ended in autumn 1959 Marten was set free. The World Jewish Congress in London protested against Merten's release from Greek detention. Seen from there Merten was a criminal and the director of this institution, A. L. Easterman, was of the opinion that Merten had gotten off too lightly with his two and a half year in prison. He demanded from the German Government to undertake everything possible to punish Merten. Should this not be done then *"another scandal affecting Germany's still far from firm standing as a democratic country."*[7]

Merten's life after his return was influenced by his fight for rehabilitation. On the one hand he had to fight against the war crime trial initiated against him. On the other hand he tried to hit the Bonn Government in the person of Adenauer's undersecretary of state, Hans Globke which let him run into the knife in Athens and had not done enough to bring him out. Besides that he set his score with the Greek Government by attacking Karamanlis and Makris.

When on 5 November 1959 Merten arrived in Munich he was arrested on the basis of a warrant of arrest of a Berlin district court of 7 October 1957 and the following day he was transferred to the Berlin Moabit prison. The examining magistrate heard him on 6, 10, 11 and

1 Spiliotis, *op. cit.*, p. 136f.
2 Deutsch-griechische Beziehungen in den 1950ziger Jahren, MfAA, A 2185, p. 19.
3 Note on a conversation between the Greek deputy Pyromaglou and the "Koll.[egen] Richter", Sektion Griechenland am 18. 11. 59. MfAA, A 12480.
4 *Ibidem*, p. 109.
5 Spiliotis, *op. cit.*, p. 138.
6 *Ibidem*, p. 140.
7 Spiliotis, *op. cit.*, p. 153.

12 November and released him from pre-trial custody on 16 November.[1] During the following months the files of the Greek trial were translated and the investigating magistrate heard eleven German witnesses. In mid-1960 he wanted to interrogate Greek witnesses in Athens but the BMJ advised against this. Thereupon in February 1961 the magistrate invited 14 Greek witnesses to Berlin but only one appeared. Now he tried on the basis of a request for judicial assistance to have witnesses questioned in Athens but this was rejected by the Greeks without giving any reason. When he invited 30 other witnesses from Athens only 4 appeared. Efforts of the German consulate in Thessaloniki to view the files there failed because they could not be found. Finally it was agreed the Greek judges would examine the witnesses in Greece a process which required an enormous amount of time. As late as April 1966 the protocols of these examinations arrived in Berlin. In May 1966 the Berlin prosecution took over the later investigations and on 4 June 1968 closed the proceedings against Merten. As his innocence had not been proven free of doubt Merten had to bear the cost of the case. The order to dismiss a case had remarkable438 pages.[2]

Merten's quarrel with Globke began already while he was waiting for his trial in Athens. He had told the court that Globke had torpedoed the transport of the Jewish women and children to Palestine. The Embassy tried to stop him from stating this: *"Nie hat jemand gesagt, das dürfen Sie nicht. Die Vertreter der Botschaft argumentierten vielmehr: Herr Merten, die Bundesrepublik gibt sich doch alle Mühe, und in vier Wochen sind Sie ja draußen. Lösen Sie doch keine neue Lawine aus."* Merten, however, made his statement. But the case became hot when Merten told this during an informal conversation with the Hessian Attorney General, Fritz Bauer. Bauer took Merten's story so seriously that he wrote a note with the reference number I Ar/26/60.[3]

This, however, was not enough for Merten. He addressed the Hamburg newspaper *Hamburger Echo*, which was close to SPD. The newspaper published his story in an article series from 12 September to 3 October. The article of 12 September contained the story how Globke hindered the transport of the Jewish women and children to Palestine. On 29 September the *Hamburger Echo* published a letter by Globke on the first page which allegedly confirmed Merten's story as the author of the written series. On 28 September DER SPIEGEL repeated the accusations against Globke.[4] But Globke was not content to write that letter to the editor. Together with Adenauer he pressed charges against Merten because of slandering and wrong accusations. Obviously Globke also wanted revenge. Before however Merten could be heard by the Frankfurt court he had to appear in the prosecutor's office in Bonn and was heard.[5] In an interview with *DIE ZEIT* Globke again denied everything.[6] The trial began as late as October 1965 but it was adjourned out of unknown reasons for an indefinite time.[7] Whether the trial was resumed before Merten's death in September 1971 is unknown to me.

There is other authoritative proof for Merten's statement that Globke torpedoed the salvage of the 10,000 Jewish women and children. On the other side Globke's assertion that had been close to the 20th July movement was scarcely credible. Merten's statement were certainly an act of revenge because Bonn had done almost nothing to free him from the Greek prison.

1 ZStL 508 AR-Z139/59 Prozessgeschichte, p. 3f.
2 *Ibidem*, pp. 4-8.
3 "Globke. Ein unbedeutender Mann" *Der Spiegel* 8 (15. Februar 1961), p.23.
4 "Kriegsverbrechen Griechenland. Ihr Onkel Konstantin" *Der Spiegel* 40 (28. September 1960), p. 32.
5 "Globke. Ein unbedeutender Mann" *Der Spiegel* 8 (15. Februar 1961), p.22.
6 "Globke und die Juden" *Die Zeit* 8 (17. Februar 1961).
7 "Merten-Prozeß vertagt" *Frankfurter Rundschau* (24. Oktober 1965).

Merten's report about K. Karamanlis and D. Makris as well as the latter's wife Doxoula Leontidou has a similar character . On 17 September 1960 the *Hamburger Echo* published the following story which was certainly inspired by Merten: On 23 November 1942 Doxoula allegedly said to Merten that two day s later the Gorgopotamos railway bridge would be blown up. Most probably Merten invented this story because from whom could the young woman have learned about the secret operation *Harling* the blowing up of the bridge an SOE commando operation in cooperation with ELAS and EDES? Moreover the bridge was in the Italian zone of occupation. Then followed a passage even less credible: Merten allegedly knew *"dass Doxoulas Onkel, Konstantin, in Athen nicht nur in Politik, sondern nebenher auch 'in Nachrichten machte'. Und zwar in doppelter Funktion: Einmal als Angehöriger der Widerstandsbewegung, dann als 'Vertrauensmann' des deutschen Sicherheitsdienstes. Da das gleiche auch für Doxoulas Verlobten, Makris, galt, hatte Merten der Bitte der Griechin nicht widerstehen können, die Fernmeldeleitung nach Athen zu Gesprächen mit ihm benutzen zu dürfen. 'Doch', erinnert sich Merten, 'es war nicht nur Liebesgeflüster, was damals die Drähte zittern ließ.' In Griechenland Agent der Deutschen zu sein, zahlte sich aus: Es bestand eine fest verbindliche Anordnung, die griechischen Agenten durch das liquidierte jüdische Vermögen 'entsprechend' zu entschädigen."*[1]

On 19 September the *Hamburger Echo* alleged further that Doxoula, her fiancé Makris and a lawyer from Serres, Karamanlis, whose law office did not run well, obtained on trust a silk store of a Jew worth 15,000 pounds sterling as reward for their cooperation with the SD. Allegedly they had sold the store a little later making a huge profit. During the trial in Athens Doxoula allegedly said that she had scarcely known Merten.[2] On 28 September DER SPIEGEL reported the affair also.[3]

This story allegedly was also an invention by Merten, the fact however is that Doxoula worked in Merten's office and was engaged to Makris and later married him. The statement that Karamanlis had worked for the resistance is absurd because the resistance (EAM/ELAS) was left oriented. Similarly senseless is the assertion that Karamanlis had worked for the SD. Karamanlis had always been a patriot and the allegation that he had enriched himself with Jewish stolen goods is malicious. It does not fit with his character. Karamanlis never enriched himself during his whole career as a politician. The word uncle (θείος) does not necessarily describe a kinship relation it was used to describe a close friend of a family the German pet name is "Nennonkel".

The articles in the *Hamburger Echo* and in *Der Spiegel* caused a great excitement in Athens. Deputies asked the government what they intended to do against the defamation. The AA in Bonn declared in its *Bulletin* without prior contacting the two press organs that the articles contained untrue claims and gross insults of the Greek Prime Minister. However the AA did not mention the content of the articles. The Greek Government threatened to file a complaint against the *Hamburger Echo*. However, Merten repeated his accusations against Doxoula in a letter to the *Hamburger Echo* which was published: She had worked in his office 18 months and then until March 1944 as his personal interpreter. In the trial in Athens, however, she had said under oath that she had briefly seen him only twice.[4]

---

1 Claus Menzel, "Wenn Eichmann auspackt" *Hamburger Echo* (17. September 1960), p. 10.
2 *Ibidem* (19. September 1960), p. 10.
3 "Kriegsverbrechen Griechenland. Ihr Onkel Konstantin" *Der Spiegel* 40 (28. September 1960), p. 34.
4 Claus Menzel, "Die griechische Regierung droht mit Strafantrag gegen das 'Hamburger Echo'" *Hamburger Echo* (29. September 1960), pp. 1 und 2.

On 30 September the *Hamburger Echo* reported on the first page that the series of articles had triggered a governmental crisis in Athens and a gagging order had been issued on the Greek press: On 19 September the Athens prosecutor had warned all newspapers appearing in the capital to not reprint the articles of *the Echo* and the Spiegel. If they did the police would confiscate the papers. When on 21 September the conservative paper *Estia* dared to do it the Prime Minister had no other choice than to distance himself from the prosecution's act. The EDA asked the Government to dispel the doubts.[1] On 3 October it was learned that minister Makris had brought *Hamburger Echo, Der Spiegel* and Merten to court in Athens.[2]

On 12 October *Der Spiegel* published a press statement of the Greek Ambassador Ypsilantis which spoke of *"ungeheuerlichen und verleumderischen"* accusations in the articles which "hinterhältigen Zwecke dienten, Gespinste eines krankhaften Hirns sind,." He denied statements which had not been mentioned in the articles but he did not utter one word at the real accusations and the facts mentioned in the articles. *Der Spiegel* listed them again and stated regarding Doxoula's statement under oath in Athens that the Greeks suffered of a weak capacity of remembering. As a proof of their closer acquaintance *Der Spiegel* published the page of a photo album, which she had given to Merten as a present on Christmas 1942, with her handwritten dedication. *Der Spiegel* further proved that the official dementi of the Athens Government consisted from the dementis of the AA and of Ypsilantis.[3]

The Spiegel author amused himself on the fact that Makris had filed his accusation against the German press in Athens though he knew that a court in Athens could do nothing there against the German press. Merten on the other side had filed his accusation against Doxoula via the Greek General Consulate the responsible law enforcement agency in Greece. In Athens Georgios Papandreou, a politician of the opposition, commented this as: *"Falls Merten seine Beziehungen zu Frau Makris nachweise, brauchten keine weiteren Prozesse mehr geführt werden. Dann müsse das Kabinett Karamanlis abtreten."*[4]

It is known that neither minister Makris nor the cabinet resigned. However on 10 November 1961 the Athenian district court condemned Merten to four years and the editorial journalists of *Hamburger Echo* and *Spiegel* to two years prison in absentia. Makris was to receive 70,000 Drachmae (about 9,300 DM) compensation. Makris had brought 35 witnesses to the court of which many could only say that they did not know anything of the collaboration of Makris or his present wife.[5] A different outcome could not be expected. Makris knew why h went to court in Greece and not in the Federal Republic.

Resumé of the Merten Case

After his return Merten to Germany Merten submitted to the district office of Berlin Schöneberg an application of compensation for his "Greek passiontide" which was decided positively in summer 1961. Prisoners of war who returned after many years after the end of the war from the Soviet Union received such payments. On 4 August 1961 Merten received a first instalment of 300 DM per months.[6] In 1962 he submitted another application that in case of his death his wife and his son should received a surviving dependants' pension. The Berlin

1 *Ibidem* (30. September 1960), p. 1.
2 *Ibidem* (3. Oktober 1960).
3 "Presse. Griechenland. Dementeritis praecox" *Der Spiegel* 42 (12. Oktober 1960), pp. 39-41. Merten said that in the album was a photo, which showed him and the other three protagonists. This photo was never published.
4 *Ibidem*, p. 41; Spyros Linardatos, *Apo tonemfylio sti chounta*, IV, (Athens: Papazisis, 1986), p. 561. There one finds critical comments by Pasalidis, Venizelos, Tsirimokos und Markezinis.
5 "Rückspiegel" *Der Spiegel* 32 (22. November 1961).
6 "Rückspiegel" *Der Spiegel* 32 (2. August 1961).

administrative tribunal rejected this at first but then an extrajudicial compromise was found.[1] Max Merten died on 21 September 1971 at the age of 60 years.

The Merten case has nothing to do with justice. Here not criminal activities were expiated, Merten was not a war criminal. The Merten case was a political one. Of the German war criminals which had terrorized the Greeks not one was punished by the German judiciary. In Greece also only a few military were convicted (Andrae) and another few were executed (Müller, Bräuer) but only right after the end of the war There was no interest in numerous trials which would cost a lot, and would block the normal work of the judiciary for a long time. The condemnation of the war criminals was left to the Federal Republic. But from the very beginning Greece expected for the suspension of the trials, a financial trade-off in the beginning the buying of tobacco Greece's main export product.

However with the signing of the London Debt Agreement of 1953 the prospect for reparations sank. When in 1957 the Yugoslavs received tarnished reparations of 300 million DM Greece demanded the same amount. When Germany delayed the negotiations the persecution of the war criminals was reactivated. The only one who fell into the trap was Max Merten. He became a kind of hostage to press through the Greek demands. When Bonn declared its readiness to pay 200 million DM tarnished as an investment credit Karamanlis promised to set Merten free immediately after the end of the trial.

The trial was dealt with by a military court. As a civilian court the judges would have been obliged to check the truth of the statements of the witnesses of the prosecution. This would certainly have led to a much milder judgement if not even an acquittal. By the unchecked statements of the witnesses of the prosecution Merten could be stylised as a war criminal par excellence. The statements of the defence witnesses could be neglected. Thus Merten was sentenced to 25 years of prison. The high politicization of the case hindered Merten's release right after the end of the trial.

This was favourable for the Greek Government because in the meantime the negotiation of the general agreement of the compensation of the Jews moved forward and Merten's release could be used as a means of pressure in these negotiations. When the negotiations were on the way to the home stretch Merten was released. Thus Merten was used as a bargaining chip in both negotiations. Spiliotis is fully right when she writes: Merten *"war das Faustpfand der Griechen für ihre Option auf Entschädigungszahlungen."*[2]

The analysis of the accusations against Merten showed in the this chapter, that he was no war criminal and no anti-Semite. Of course one can accuse him that he did not oppose signing the orders which Wisliceny brought with him. However only a few would have dared to reject this because the consequences would certainly have been ackward if not even dangerous. The only thing which one can accuse Merten of is his lack of civil courage. Thus a certain amount of moral guilt can be stated at most. It is known that the valuable furniture of the deported Jews was brought to Germany and given to bombed out people but they did not become Merten's privat ownership. The accusation that Merten enriched himslef with the fortunes of the Jews cannot be proved.

Merten as an administrative officer had a difficult post but he did his job honestly. Generally speaking one can state that Merten did his work as administrative officer correctly.

Merten's double revenge actions after his release can be understood however, the way how he fortified his accusations with dubious accusations show that his was a refined lawyer who

1 *Tagesspiegel* (23 Februar 1973).
2 Spiliotis, *op. cit.*, p. 155.

attacks his opponent with all kinds of tricks. By his attack on Globke and the Greek trio he entered a terrain which would have been better avoided. He behaved ineptly and naive and resorted to the same level as the others.

Spiliotis formulated the behaviour of Greece and the Federal Republic excellently when she wrote: *"Die Handlungsmaximen der deutschen und griechischen Entscheidungsträger zeichneten sich nicht nur durch einen Mangel an 'Rechtsgefühl' aus; vielmehr offenbarte sich ein Maß an moralischer Anspruchslosigkeit, das dem Selbstverständnis der Bundesrepublik, aber auch Griechenlands als 'firm standing democracies' Hohn sprach. Mit der politischen Lösung der Kriegsverbrecherfrage wurde vielleicht die Widerannäherung beider Länder nach dem Krieg forciert; doch der Preis dafür war die 'Suspendierung der Gerechtigkeit'."*[1] One can only agree with this statement. Indeed in this case injustice was done in order to achieve the aim, by making an "innocent" a "war criminal" because one did not have any real German war criminal.

The accusation that Merten had been an evil war criminal has remained in the Greek public to this day. During the recent financial crisis it was revived in order to prove that the Germans are still Nazis and were aiming at the erection of a fourth Reich.

1 *Ibidem*, p. 158.

THE MYTH OF THE COMMUNIST REVOLUTION IN DECEMBER 1944

Die Dekemvriana

In Greek and English language historiography of the Cold War period on Greek history in WWI the events in December 1944 in Athens were a Communist Revolution. In order to hinder an absorption of Greece by the Soviet Union Churchill had to intervene. He saved Greece's freedom This is the myth but what is the truth?

The Historical Background

In order to be able to understand the developments which lead to the December events it is necessary to have a look at Greek history in the 19th century. In 1821 the Greeks rose against the Ottoman Empire and in a years long bloody fight they reached their freedom. However when in 1830 they wanted to form a republic the Holy Alliance intervened and imposed the Bavarian Otto von Wittelsbach not as king by grace of god but by grace of the great powers. He was to rule the country as governor of the great powers and keep the country on a course which suited the great powers. Three of the great powers - England, France and Russia - considered themselves as the protecting powers of Greece. In 1862 King Otto, who during the Crimean War had followed a policy which did not please the great powers, was removed from his throne and replaced by a member of the house of Schleswig-Holstein-Sonderburg-Glücksburg. At the same time the number of the protective powers was reduced to one - Britain.[1]

From now on Greece was a British client state and the new monarch played the role of a British viceroy who determined the Greek politicians to steer a pro-British course. This functioned quite well because of the clientelistic character of the Greek internal politics. If a Greek monarch turned himself against the protective power, as Constantine I did in WWI the protective power made sure that he quickly lost his throne.

The reasons for Britain's interest were from the beginning of a geostrategical nature. Already in 1841 the British ambassador in Athens, Sir Edmund Lyons, had formulated the principles crystal clear: *"A Greece truly independent is an absurdity. Greece is Russian or she is English; and since she must not be Russian, it is necessary that she be English."*[2] Greece was an important link of the British life line from England over Gibraltar, Malta, Cyprus, Egypt and Aden to India. Alone by her existence Greece kept the Russians away from the Mediterranean and from the Aegean islands one could control the straits of Bosporus and Dardanelles. Thus Greece had become an important location of the global conflict between Russia and Britain in the 19th century which was then called the great game. And this game continued in the 2oth century though slightly altered. For the British policy this meant: As long as the British Empire existed Greece had to remain a British client state at any cost. Greek politicians, conservatives and liberals alike, had understood this and aligned their policy accordingly: at times they subordinated Greek interests to the British ones.[3] Any politician

---

1 Emanuel Turczynski, *Sozial- und Kulturgeschichte Griechenlands im 19. Jahrhundert. Von der Hinwendung zu Europa bis zu den ersten Olympischen Spielen der Neuze*it (Mannheim: Bibliopolis, 2003), *passim.*

2 Leften S. Stavrianos, *Greece: American Dilemma and Opportunity* (Chicago: Henry Regnery, 1952), opposite title page.

3 Their maxim was: Ti thelei o xenos paragontas? What does the foreign factor want?

who disregarded this risked a clash with the King. However this rarely happened and thus a stable system formed itself which functioned until WWII.[1]

However in WWII developments occurred which challenged the clientelistic dependency. Firstly, a resistance movement came into being which wanted a postwar republic and an equal partnership with Britain and, secondly, the Soviets advanced to the Balkans and threatened the British life line.

The desire for the formation of a postwar republic had been provoked by King Georg II himself. He had returned to his throne after a rather dubious plebiscite and had sworn to respect the constitution of the country. However when in 1936 the authetic democratic elections produced a parliamentary stalemate situation and the communist which had gained 5 percent of the seats in parliament became the tipping point of the scales when forming the government. George II believed or at least pretended to believe that a communist revolution was threatening Greece and therefore on 4 August 1936 he signed the decrees which abolished democracy and made general Metaxas dictator. This was a clear breach of the constitution by the king, for which the people never forgave him.[2]

Since the king continued to steer a pro-British course London was not alarmed when the Germanophile dictator Metaxas began to erect a modified copy of the German Fascism. He disempowered the politicians of the old clientelistic parties and orientated the clients onto himself. He described his regime as follows: "*Griechenland erhielt am 4. August eine antikommunistische Herrschaft, eine antiparlamentarische Herrschaft, eine totalitäre Herrschaft, eine Herrschaft auf der Basis der Bauern und Arbeiter und folglich eine antiplutokratische Herrschaft.*"[3] In January 1941 he wrote in his *Tetralin ton Skepseon* (notebook for thoughts): "*Sicher hatte es [Griechenland] keine besondere Herrschaftspartei. Aber das ganze Volk war die Partei, außer den unverbesserlichen Kommunisten und den reaktionären Anhängern der 'Alten Parteien'.*"[4] Metaxas considered the whole population as his clientele; this may be called clientelistic fascism.[5]

Though the regime imitated its German example with parades and deployments but it was clear that the 4 August system was a poor people's version of Fascism.[6] The breakup of the old clientelistic networks had an undesired aftereffect. It created the precondition for the people's resistance during the occupation. When Greece was occupied the clientelistic network of Metaxas fell into bits The leaderless sub-networks could be integrated into the new network of the national resistance.

---

1 Heinz Richter, "Zwischen Tradition und Moderne: Die politische Kultur Griechenlands,." in: Peter Reichel (ed.), *Politische Kultur in Westeuropa, Bürger und Staaten in der Europäischen Gemeinschaft* (Bonn: Bundeszentrale für politische Bildung, 1984), pp. 145-166.

2 Heinz Richter, *Griechenland zwischen Revolution und Konterrevolution (1936-1946)* (Frankfurt: EVA, 1973); Idem, *Geschichte Griechenlands im 20. Jahrhundert* Band 1 *1900-1939* (Ruhpolding: Rutzen, 2015), pp. 297-342.

3 Ioannis Metaxas, *To prosopiko tou imerologio*, IV (Athen: Ikaros, 1960), p. 553.

4 *Ibidem.*

5 Heinz Richter, "Clientelstic Fascism", in: Harry Cliadakis, *Fascism in Greece. The Metaxas Dictatorship* (Ruhpolding: Rutzen, 2015), pp. 135-140.

6 Spyros Linardatos, *Η Τεταρτη Αυγουστου* (Athen: Themelio, 1966); Heinz Richter, "Aspekte der griechischen Zeitgeschichte", *Aus Politik und Zeitgeschichte* 14/15 (1. April 1988), p. 27; idem, "Griechenland im Zweiten Weltkrieg: Eroberung - Okkupation - Kollaboration - Widerstand - Exil - Befreiung und Bürgerkrieg", in: Karl Giebeler, Heinz A. Richter, Reinhard Stupperich (eds.), *Versöhnung ohne Wahrheit? Deutsche Kriegsverbrechen in Griechenland im Zweiten Weltkrieg. Beiträge einer Tagung am 27.-28. Oktober 2000 in der Evangelischen Akademie Bad Boll* (Mannheim, Möhnesee: Bibliopolis, 2001), pp. 12-30.

In foreign policy the regime steered a swing course. George II steered a course of reassurance with Britain and Metaxas counted on ideological friendship with Berlin and with Rome and dreamed of an international fascist solidarity. He was bitterly disappointed when the fascist Italy attacked the fascist Greece on 28 October 1940.

As is well known the Italian attack failed and the Greeks pushed the Italian aggressor far back into Albania. Hitler who was preparing operation Barbarossa was afraid of an intervention of Britain in Greece which could endanger his plans in a double sense. First, the British might bomb the Rumanian oilfields from Greece and second. They might open a Balkan front as in WWI. In order to remove this thread from the flanks the Wehrmacht occupied Yugoslavia and Greece in April 1941.

The Time of the Occupation

During the ensuing three years until October 1944 Greece encountered ths same fate as all occupied countries in Europe. There were collaborationist governments, which became more and more tools of their occupiers. A broad resistance movement came into being which however in Greece was split into diverse political groups which fought each other. And there was also a government in exile under George II in Cairo and London which alienated itself from the reality in Greece.[1]

The formation of the resistance movement was favoured by two factors: First, by the famine in winter 1941/42,[2] which excited the people to rebellion, and, second, the capital psychological mistake which Hitler made, when he allocated the occupation of Greece to the Italians who had been beaten by the Greeks in Albania and to the Bulgarian who were considered by the Greeks as hereditary enemies.[3] The various resistance groups which came into being had all one thing in common: they were republican oriented. Royalist resistance did not exist. This is true for EDES which in the beginning was left-liberal republican oriented, and leftist EAM/ELAS. Both groups demanded a plebiscite on the form of government and that the king would not return before it was held.[4]

Churchill's Policy in 1943

In London in the beginning nobody was interested in the political opinions of the Greek resistance movements. For Churchill it was enough that they attacked the occupation forces and committed troops. In April 1943 Churchill was warned by the chief of the British Military Mission, Brigadier Myers, for the first time: Should the king return before a plebiscite there would be a civil war. London should make a declaration that the British Government did not intend to restore the King by force.[5]

---

1 On the occupation time Hagen Fleischer, *Im Kreuzschatten der Mächte. Griechenland 1941-1944* (Frankfurt: Lang, 1986); Mark Mazower, *Inside Hitler's Greece. The Experience of Occupation 1941-44* (New Haven: Yale University Press, 1993); Richter, *Revolution und Konterrevolution*, passim.

2 On the faminet s. the chapter in this book.

3 Mark Mazower, "Greece and the New Europe 1941-1944", in: Philipp Carabott (ed.), *Greece and Europe in the Modern Period* (London: King's College, 1995). p. 85.

4 On the resistance Fleischer, *Kreuzschatten*, p. 397ff; C. M. Woodhouse, *Apple of Discord. a Survey of Recent Greek Politics in their International Setting* (London: Hutchinson, 1948); Hagen Fleischer, "Griechenland - Der Krieg geht weiter", in: Ulrich Herbert u. Axel Schildt (eds.), *Kriegsende in Europa. Vom Beginn des deutschen Machtzerfalls bis zur Stabilisierung der Nachkriegsordnung 1944-1948* [2](Essen: Klartext, 1999), pp. 173-5; Richter, *Revolution und Konterrevolution, passim.*

5 Richter, *Revolution und Konterrevolution,* p. 284

Churchill was interested in this opinion. He thought that the Greek king could be restored in the context of a general allied landing in the Balkans. In March 1943 he guaranteed George II his return.[1] It was British policy that the King returned in any case and that in Greece a "string administration" would be formed.[2] Though during the Conference in Quebec the Balkan landing became questionable Churchill did not give up his plan to bring the king back accompanied by British troops.[3]

The Italian change of sides in September 1943 made a landing more and more improbable and led to a strengthening of the Greek resistance. Churchill recognized that the restoration of the monarchy could only be achieved by the use of force. At the end of September he gave orders: *"Should the Germans evacuate Greece we must certainly be able to send 5,000 British troops with armoured cars and Bren gun carriers into Athens.[...] The troops need not be organised to contend with more than rioting."*[4] This was the decision for an armed intervention in Greece after the withdrawal of the Germans. Although brigadier Myers in October 1943 proposed an alternative course which might have lead to a peaceful solution Churchill did not change his course.[5] Churchill justified his hard course to the public by alleging against better intelligence that after the retreat of the Germans the communists would take over.

Though it is true that the communists played a major role in the resistance - ELAS had been founded by the people's front - but they controlled the mass movement of the resistance far less than one could have assumed. The EAM united all progressive forces from the Liberals to the Communists. And the Communist Party changed from a cadre party to a mass party. Towards the end of the occupation its ideology was similar to that of the Euro-Communists in the 1970s. EAM and its sub-organizations were a broad popular movement allegedly it had 1,5 million members - it had the following aims: Liberations of the country from the Fascist occupants, for the time after war in foreign policy national independence was the aim, i.e. the old clientelistic relationship to Great Britain should end and be replaced by a partnership based on equality. In internal policy a democratic and socially just republic with democratic structure was the aim, i.e. the country should be Europeanized and the basic evil, clientelism would be removed.[6] A Communist takeover was not intended as is proven.[7]

And it is exactly here where the problem was. Churchill considered the leaders of the resistance as "miserable banditti" or "communist troublemakers" who in case of doubt could be brought to reason by a show of strength.[8] He did not understand or did not want to understand that the Greek resistance i.e. EAM was a broad popular movement. In his eyes the only guarantor for a pro-British policy of Greece was the King. The idea that a Greek republic might follow a pro-British policy did not agree with his thinking. Therefore after the liberation of Greece there would be a conflict.

---

1 Imanouil Tsouderos, *Anomalies sti Mesi Anatoli* (Athen: Aetos, 1945), p. 67

2 *Ibidem.*

3 Winston Churchill, *The Second World War,* X (London: Cassell, 1964), p. 188

4 *Ibidem*, p. 189.

5 Richter, *Revolution und Konterrevolution*, p. 320f.

6 Heinz Richter, "Die griechische kommunistische Partei (KKE) 1944 - 1947: Von der Massenpartei zur Kaderpartei", in: Dietrich Staritz und Hermann Weber (eds.), *Einheitsfront Einheitspartei. Kommunisten und Sozialdemokraten in Ost- und Westeuropa 1944 - 1948* (Köln: Verlag Wissenschaft und Politik, 1989), pp.453 - 468; Idem, "Die Entwicklung der griechischen Linken 1918-1996", in: Patrick Moreau, et al. (eds.), *Der Kommunismus in Westeuropa* (Landsberg: Olzog Verlag, 1998), pp. 131-166.

7 On this the former general secretary of KKE Grigoris Farakos, *O ELAS kai I Exousia* (Athen: Ellinika Grammata, 2000) 2 volumes.

8 Churchill, *op. cit.*, X, p. 195.

Churchill's Policy of Spheres of Interest

In September 1943 Churchill had given the order to restore the monarchy by force after the German retreat. In spring 1944 the chance came to bring the Greek forces in exile which in their majority were republican oriented on the "right" course. In occupied Greece a counter-government, the PEEA, had been formed in the liberated mountains. This had caused demonstrations of sympathy among the Greek forces in exile. Churchill declared these manifestations as a communist mutiny and ordered to clean the force of all Leftists and Republicans. From now on the Greece forces were hard-royalist and fanatical anti-communist.[1] In the context of the conference in Lebanon in which representatives of the resistance and the government in exile negotiated about a government of national unity Churchill succeeded via the British Ambassador Leeper in making Georgios Papandreou prime minister, who was in every sense ready to collaborate with the British.

Until this moment the Soviet Union had not paid any attention to the events in Greece. The establishment of the PEEA and the abolition of the so-called mutiny caused Moscow, the first time to openly mingle in Greek affairs. The TASS news agency published an article which was reprinted by all Soviet news papers. In it the Greek Government and thus implicitly Britain was massively criticised. On 16 April Churchill protested in a message to foreign minister Molotov: *"I am sure you would not allow such things to go on in the Soviet armies or among forces which you might control. I therefore hope that TASS may be told to leave off this agitation."*[2]

In his replay of 22 April Molotov asked for precise information about what had happened in Greece and then he mentioned Rumania and asked for British support of the British support in the secret peace negotiations which were going on since the middle of March 1944.[3] It was obvious that Molotov wanted to establish a link between Greece and Rumania. In a second letter of the end of April Molotov became even more outspoken: The British controlled the Greek developments *"in the most direct manner"* and the Soviets kept out of this but then Molotov complained that the British played a double game.[4] Since it was clear that following the the next Soviet advance Rumania and Bulgaria would fall in their hands Churchill saw a need for action.

Foreign Minister Eden was instructed to discuss the controversial topics with the Soviets. On 5 May a conversation between Eden and Soviet Ambassador Gusew in London took lace. Eden suggested *"that the Soviet Union 'should take the lead in our joint efforts to get Romania out of the war"* and regarding Greece he *"felt entitled to ask for Soviet help."* Rumania was in the Soviet *"sphere of command"*, Greece in the British.[5] Despite the cautious wording the postwar spheres of influence were negotiated. The Russians agreed to the British proposal but wanted to know whether the Americans were informed.

And exactly here was a problem. President Roosevelt and primarily the American Secretary of State Hull were against spheres of interest primarily out of economic reasons, and the British and the Russians knew this quite well because in December 1941 during the first Soviet-British negotiations regarding the form of postwar Europe, this attitude had let to failure .

---

1 On the "Mutiny" Richter, *Revolution und Konterrevolution*, p. 392-416.

2 Elizabeth Barker, "Greece in the Framework of Anglo-Soviet Relations 1941-1947," in: Marion Sarafis (ed.), *Greece: From Resistance to Civil War* (London: Spokesman, 1980), p. 22.

3 Churchill, *op. cit.*, XI, p. 64.

4 Barker, *op. cit.*, p. 22.

5 Churchill, *op. cit.*, XI, p. 64f; Barker, *op. cit.*, p. 22f.

During these talks Stalin had told Eden his ideas about spheres of interest. He mentioned areas which the Soviet Union had obtained in the Hitler-Stalin pact including Finland and Rumania. The British should obtain navy bases in Boulogne Dunkirk, in Belgium and the Netherlands and even in Denmark and Norway. Stalin mentioned other countries as well and suggested the signing of a secret pact on this. Greece was not mentioned expressis verbis but it was clear that it would be in the British sphere of interest.[1] The BBC correspondent of many years, Elizabeth Barked, commented on the negotiations:

"These exchanges show that at least in talking to Eden Stalin was entirely pragmatic, non-ideological, un-Marxist or one might even say pre-Marxist, talking in terms of buying off potential allies, bribing potential allies, and dividing up the expected spoils of victory."[2]

Eden was attired in this but had to reject it because the Americans which were in the war since Pearl Harbour in early December, rejected spheres of interest out of principle. And because of their lend-lease-agreement they might have been able to insist on their conception. Nevertheless during the British-Soviet negotiations of an alliance in spring 1942 the British agreed that the Russian-Rumanian border of 1940 should remain as it had been agreed with Hitler in 1940 by the Wiener Schiedsspruch.[3]

In view of the American position on the question of spheres of interest extreme caution was necessary. Eden instructed the British Ambassador in Washington, Halifax, to inform the Americans *"stressing that the British had 'no desire to carve up the Balkans into spheres of influence' the proposal was just 'a useful device for preventing a divergence of policy' in the area."*[4] He should stress the temporary character of such an agreement. Foreign Secretary Hull reacted rejecting the idea. An exchange of diplomatic notes between London and Washington followed,[5] in which the British constantly stressed that such an agreement should have only three months validity. Cordell Hull, however, rejected the British proposals. However, he was absent from Washington in early June and Roosevelt allowed himself to be softened up by Churchill's pestering requests.

On 12 June he agreed to the three-months-agreement. However, he stressed that Churchill should monitor that no permanent postwar spheres of interest came into being.[6] Churchill expressed his thanks and announced that he would inform the Soviet Union. Even when Hull returned to the Department of State and tried to return to his previous line Churchill managed to carry his point and Roosevelt agreed again to the three-months-agreement.

The Soviets on the other side played out their opportunity, because their armies were moving towards the Rumanian border and it was just a matter of time when they would occupy Rumania. After further diplomatic negotiations Soviets and British considered the three-months-agreement to be in force.[7] On 23 August King Michael of Rumania mad a putsch against the Rumanian fascist leader Antonescu and ended the war against the Soviet Union. However this did not hinder the Red Army from occupying the country. On 2 September Bulgaria changed sides but this did not hinder the Soviet Union from declaring war on Bulgaria and occupying Sofia in mid-September. The occupation of Yugoslavia and Hungary was only a question of time. Eden saw that the three-month-agreement was about to expire and only the Soviets had benefited from it.

1 Barker, *op. cit.*, p. 16.
2 *Ibidem.*
3 *Ibidem*, p. 17.
4 *Ibidem*, p. 25.
5 Richter, *Revolution und Konterrevolution*, p. 462.
6 *Ibidem.*
7 *Ibidem*, p. 464.

But the Soviets stuck to the agreement and supported the British: At the end of July they sent a military mission to the lead of EAM/ELAS which induced it to cooperate and enter the government of national unity. Thus the peaceful return of the government in exile to Greece was assured. On 21 September the British informed the Soviets that in a few days British troops would enter Greece. The Soviets were reminded of Britain's special interest in Greece and the latter express the hope that the Soviets would not send troops to Greece. Two days later Wyschinski conformed that the Soviets considered the three-months-agreement in force and that there was no intention to send troops to Greece.[1]

The Percentage Agreement
Churchill and Eden saw that the Soviets were ready to respect the temporary sphere of interest. Why should it not be possible to transfer this concept into the post-war time without any limit of time? The South-African Prime Minister Ian Smuts warmly supported this idea. On 26 September in a telegram he stressed the importance of Greece for the Empire. The plan to form after the war the UNO was quite nice but it was more important that the Empire emerge stronger out of the war.[2]

In the meantime Churchill had finished his military preparations. On 29 August he ordered: *"It is most desirable to strike out of the blue without any preliminary crisis."*[3] After the German retreat 1,500 parachutists should occupy Athens, the airport and the Piraeus.. They should be followed by 10,000 regular troops with tanks, artillery and armoured vehicles. *"The operation must be regarded as one of reinforced diplomacy and policy rather than an actual campaign, and that it is to be confined to Athens."*[4] Even the Americans were ready to provide the necessary air transport room. Additionally four squadrons of air planes should be transferred to Athens.

As the retreat of the Germans from Greece and Yugoslavia was delayed Churchill found time to safeguard his plans diplomatically. He saw that Stalin was building a sphere of interest and decided to do the same even if he had to deceive Roosevelt.[5] The chance to do this came in early October. In September Churchill had suggested a meeting of the big three in Moscow. Roosevelt had agreed but he could not keep the appointment because he was in the middle of the election campaign for his fourth presidency. Ambassador Harriman was to replace him. Churchill agreed but Roosevelt would certainly have nothing against *"private tête-à-tête between me and Uncle Joe or Anthony and Molotov"*. Such meetings were prolific and he would inform him about everything.[6]

Already on the first evening in Moscow (9 October 1944) after a dinner for four (Stalin, Molotow, Eden, Churchill) the notorious percentage agreement was concluded by which the Balkan was divided into permanent spheres of interest.[7] The agreement had Scarcely been accepted by Stalin when Churchill got cold feet. He was afraid of a clash with the Americans and criticism in the House of Commons therefore it was decided to keep the agreement totally

---

1 Barker, *op. cit.*, p. 27.
2 Churchill, *op. cit.*, XI, p. 187
3 *Ibidem*, p. 251
4 *Ibidem*, p. 98
5 Barker, *op. cit.*, p. 27.
6 Churchill, *op. cit.*, XI, p. 194.
7 *Ibidem*, XI, p. 201

secret and inform the Americans only very vaguely.[1] But the agreement was to be in force permanently.[2]

The meaning of the percentage agreement for the Balkans is clear. Rumania and Bulgaria would belong to the Soviet sphere of interest. Yugoslavia would be neutralized and Greece in the British sphere of interest. Stalin gave Churchill a free hand in Greece and expected the same in his sphere. Thus Churchill needed only to subdue EAM/ELAS in order to return to the status quo ante, i.e. the old clientelistic state of dependency.

The Return of the Government in Exile

The Soviets made the Greek Left enter the Papandreou Government in early September. The PEEA was dissolved and in the so-called Cazerta agreement ELAS put itself under the command of the British intervention troops general Ronald Scobie. In order not to endanger anything at the last moment the British made it clear to George II that he had to stay outside Greece for the time being.[3] However , during a conversation with Papandreou Churchill made it clear that he was determined to restore the monarchy and rejected the proposed regency.[4]

On 18 October the return of the government in exile went off without a hitch. If the left had wanted to hinder the return it could have done this easily since it controlled 90 percent of Greece at the time of the liberation. During the next weeks it seemed that the road to the postwar time would be peaceful. Churchill said that as a high price had been paid for the freedom of action in Greece one should not shy away from using the troops. *"I fully expect a clash with EAM, and we must not shrink from it, provided the ground is well chosen."*[5]

Despite all stirring there was a problem: The Left was cooperative and ready for compromise and not aiming at a conflict. There was only one critical point: the question of the demobilising the partisan units and the creation of a new army. The Left was ready to demobilize its own forces but at the same time it was determined not to allow the new army to become a party army of the Right. Therefore it demanded a general demobilization including the exile forces and a total rebuild. At the end of November after long negotiations a reasonable compromise was found but on orders of Churchill and Papandreou it was undermined. Under protest the EAM ministers resigned on 1 December. Thus the doom began.[6]

On 3 December the Greek police gunned down an unarmed demonstration on Syntagma Square. Embarrassing was that this happened in front of the eyes and cameras of the world press and these reported accordingly.[7] Even the conservative London *Times* called this a fascist action.[8] On 4 December a general strike and a morning demonstration took plae for those killed the day before took place. Papandreou washed his hands of it and was ready to resign so that the leader of the liberals Sofoulis could become prime minister.[9] Thus there was a last chance to solve the crisis peacefully, but now Churchill intervened.

---

1 Barker, *op. cit.*, p. 28.

2 Heinz Richter, *Britisch Intervention in Greece: Form Varkiza to Civil War, Februar 1945 - August 1946* (London: The Merlin Press, 1986), p. VIII. Idem, *Griechenland 1945/46: Die British Intervention* (Ruhpolding: Rutzen, 2016).

3 Richter, *Revolution und Konterrevolution*, p. 495.

4 *Ibidem*, p. 497.

5 *Churchill, op. cit.*, XI, p. 254.

6 Heinz Richter, "The Battle of Athens and the Rôle of the British", in: Marion Sarafis (ed.), *Greece: From Resistance to Civil War* (Nottingham: Spokesman, 1980), p. 78-90.

7 Dimitri Kessel, *Ellada tou '44* (Athen: Ammos, 1994).

8 Michael Foot, *Aneuran Bevan. A Biography,* I (London, 1962), p. 478.

9 Richter, *Revolution und Konterrevolution*, p. 521.

The Dekemvriana

Remembering Arthur Balfour's "don't hesitate-to-shoot-telegram" during an Irish rebellion in the 1880s Churchill formulated his instructions. He forbade the change of government in Greece and instructed Scobie: *"Do not however hesitate to act as if you were in a conquered city where a local rebellion is in progress. [...] We have to hold and dominate Athens. It should be a great thing for you to succeed in this without bloodshed if possible, but also with bloodshed if necessary."*[1] These were isolated decisions which did not even have the blessing of the Cabinet.

During the next days the reserve-ELAS of Athens attacked the police stations avoiding a direct confrontation with the British. Thy, however, mingled more and more into the inner-Greek fighting. After 12 December the fighting assumed a double character: It was a civil war between the Greek Left and the Greek Right and a war between the British and the Athenian reserve ELAS into which even the RAF intervened.[2]

The armed intervention led to massive critique in the House of Commons. Churchill's intervention policy after WWI was remembered and his course was rejected.[3] Of the 680 member of the House only 297 voted for Churchill's policy, 30 voted against but more than half of the members abstained from voting.[4] In Washington President Roosevelt was furious and recommended the formation of a regency. From Moscow, however, not one critical word was heard. Stalin stood by the percentage agreement. Churchill on the other side spoke in his telegrams to Stalin of a Trotskyte rebellion which made it easier for Stalin to stay neutral.

Until Christmas 1944 British and international pressure of Churchill became so strong that be felt obliged to go to Athens and to seek there for a political solution.[5] In order to bring the Greek bourgeois camp on his side again Churchill agreed to the establishment of a regency until a plebiscite would be held. But the fighting in Athens continued despite of these talks. Only on 11 January was an armistice concluded which was followed by the peace treaty of Varkiza in February.

The Peace Treaty of Varkiza

This treaty was a fair compromise which was concluded between the opponents of the civil war and guaranteed by the British. If its text and its spirit had been respected a lasting peace and reconciliation would have been possible. However during the ensuing twelve months a counter-revolutionary wave of unimaginable strength hit Greece which reversed the balance of power totally. Greece was the only country in Europe in which collaborators were not punished but rewarded and where membership in the leftist resistance movement was considered a crime and pursued.[6] In early 1946 a British MP got the impression that Greece was becoming a Fascist state.[7] All this happened with the approval of the British. The British Ambassador acted as "high commissioner" in the "British protectorate, both terms literally

1 Churchill, *op. cit.*, XI, p. 256.

2 Heinz Richter, "Die Royal Air Force und die Dekemvriana", *THETIS* 3 (1996), pp. 231-242.

3 Alex P. Schmid, *Churchills privater Krieg, Intervention und Konterrevolution im Russischen Bürgerkrieg, 1918-1920* (Zürich: Atlantis, 1974).

4 *House of Commons Debates*, Vol. 406, col. 1010.

5 Richter, *Revolution und Konterrevolution*, pp. 548ff.

6 *"During 1945 membership of the resistance movement had become to be regarded as a political crime and collaboration with the Germans against Communism a political virtue."* Woodhouse, *op. cit.*, p. 256.

7 Leslie J. Solley, *Greece. The Facts* (London, 1946), p. 14f.

stem from the files of the Foreign Office of that time.[1] Leeper replace the Greek prime minister as he like. When in spring 1945 he had doubts because of incredibly brutal insults of the Right against the Left Churchill rebuked him: Communism is a worse crime than collaboration with the Nazis.[2]

Churchill's intervention in Greece was one of the reasons why he was not reelected in summer 1945. The British voter was afraid of further interventionist adventures. However the change to the Labour Party did not change anything. Bevin's foreign policy did not differ from Churchill's: His anti-communism was even stronger and his aim was the protection of the life line of the British Empire. The Greek Right interpreted this as an approval of their repression course and intensified it.

The events in December 1944 were complex On the one hand they were a civil war between the Right and the Left. Its aims were reform of the Greek state from its roots or the restoration of the old clientelistic system. On the other hand it was a British intervention to restore the status quo ante. However one could interpret it as the first hot round in the escalating cold war: a paradigmatic case for Stalin's later course of action in Eastern Europe.

In early 1946 the persecuted Left began to fight back. Now the process of force and counterforce began which led to the outback of the Civil War I summer 1946. When in spring 1946 a delegation of the Greek CP (KKE) visited Moscow and asked Stalin for advice he advised the Greek comrades to participate in the impending elections and to integrate into the political system.[3] In other words: Stalin adhered to the percentage agreement, Greece belonged to the British sphere of interest. This again became visible during the Greek Civil War; Stalin dd not lift a finger to help the Greek communists because he did not want to be drawn into a hot war with Western Powers.[4] Help for the Greek communists came only from Tito who was able to steer an independent course because of the percentage agreement.

The Greek Right emerge as victor out of the elections in March 1946 because the Liberals and Leftists boycotted the election. After a very dubious plebiscite the monarchy was restored. Obviously Greece had again become a British client state. But in winter 1946 British financial means ran short and therefore they turned to the Americans for help. The Americans were ready to help and thus in 1947 in the form of the Truman Doctrine a change of the guards to the Americans took place.[5] Dan Diner calls this a *translatio imperii*.[6] The Americans took over the traditional role of the British to keep the Russians away from the Mediterranean.

But quite in contrast to the British who themselves had intervened the Americans let the Greeks fight. They armed the Greek forces and trained them. Only very rarely they intervened directly but only to test new weapons.[7] However, after the end of the Civil War the Americans did not withdraw. They continued to keep the country under their control but in contrast to the British which had used the King to control the country the Americans used the army and the secret service. The Greek army and also the Turkish developed into a praetorian guard of the US, as Theodoros Koulumbis wrote many years ago[8] which kept the country of a pro-

---

1 The term "High Commissioner" is found this document: "Discussions on Greece at the British Embassy, Athens 15th February 1945", PRO, F.O. 371/48 257/3/19; the term "Protectorate" stems from "Relations between HMG and the Greek Government. Minutes", F.O. 371/48 256/R4385/4/19.

2 Churchill to Sir Orme Sargent on 22 April 1945. "PREM, Serial no. 382/5 0 F.O. 371/48 267R7423/4/19.

3 Mitsos Partsalidis, *Dipli apokatastasi tis ethnikis antistasis* (Athen: Themelio, 1978), p. 198.

4 *Ibidem*, p. 199.

5 On the Civil War Heinz Richter, *Griechenland 1940-1950. Die Zeit der Bürgerkriege* (Ruhpolding: Rutzen, 2012)

6 *Ibidem.*

7 Lawrence Wittner, *American Intervention in Greece, 1943-1949* (New York: Columbia UP, 1987).

8 Theodore A. Couloumbis, *Foreign Interference in Greek Politics. An Historical Perspective* (New York: Yale

American course. In case a change of course threatened e.g. in the middle of the 1960s the Americans allowed an overturn of the Papandreou Government and when his election victory threatened they did not interfere when the Greek generals prepared a coup. However it were not the generals who made the coup but the colonels who took over on 21 April 1967.

For many years the role of the US could not be described from reliable sources because the volume of "Foreign Relations of the United States" of the years 1964-68 which had been printed but the CIA blocked its distribution. It finally appeared in 2002.

Only the catastrophe of 1974 and the entry into the EU ended the traditional clientelistic relationship to its protecting power. Military interventions controlled from abroad were now excluded by the democratization of Greek politics. The implosion of the Soviet Union ended the Cold War. But the fight for spheres of interest seem to continue as the conflicts in the Near East show. If the Balkans will be spared seems insecure as was shown during the wars following the braking up of Yugoslavia. Only Greece seems to be free of such intentions.

Conclusions
The Dekemvriana were a British intervention to restore the monarchy. By this intervention Churchill deprived Greece of its only historical chance to get rid of the cancerous evil clientelism. Of course it is not absolutely sure whether a postwar government based on the resistance would have been able to ostracise clientelism out of Greek policy but it would have been at least weakened. Perhaps such a government might have moved the Greek political system closer to those of the Western European states.

On the other hand this British intervention in WWII is the first such action in a country to impose ones own political system. Stain's actions in the Balkans and in Eastern Europe did only imitate it.

UP, 1976),p. 142

REPARATIONS

The Actual Reason

In the context of the Greek financial crisis of 2011, 2012 and 2015 the Greek demands of reparations from Germany came to the boil once more. Because the debt of the Greek state amounted to 200 billions Euro the sum demanded as reparations was raised to this sum in the first two years. If Germany paid the Greek state would be free of debts. This was the opinion of some Athens newspapers. In 2015 the Greek state's debts had risen to 278,3 billion Euro and the Tsipras government demanded this sum as reparations. At a first glance this demand appeared to seem justified because Greece allegedly never received any reparations. But is it true that the German side never did pay nothing at all? This study will analyse this question.

Greece's Economic Situation After the War

The main problem of Greece was that til June 1845 there was no economic policy of the Government. If the population did not suffer another famine like in 1941 it was the result of the good work of the British Military Liaison-Organization which brought food into the country and distributed it; later the UNRRA took over this task. The economic oligarchy, however, managed to take over the distribution and by doing so earned a fortune. Additionally there was the problem of the inflation. Though the Drachmae was devaluated several times the problem was not solved. The British golden pound became the main currency which devaluated the Drachmae even further.

Kyriakos Varvaressos, the governor of the Bank of Greece fought desperately for a reform program and the increase of the taxes but the economic oligarchy blocked him successfully. Varvaresssos declared his resignation. The new governor stemmed from this oligarchy and steered a course which pleased it. He was supported by the minister of Economics who stemmed from the same clique. At the end of September total economic chaos ruled. The prices for food and the golden pound rose at a tearing pace. On 2 October Ambassador Leeper criticized Prime Minister Voulgaris for his failed economic policy. Voulgaris accepted the critique and said that only help from outside could save Greece.

Since the Greek government did not have any tax revenues it turned to the traditional means of Greek fiscal policy and applied for a 250 million Dollar credit in Washington. At the same time it spread the rumour that Greece would receive this credit.

The Export-Import Bank which was responsible for such queries rejected a credit so high. Not even a solvent borrower could have received such a sum. But the bank war ready to support a concrete programs of Greece with 25 million Dollars. The State Department informed Ambassador MacVeagh accordingly. However first of all the talk about a 250 million credit should be stopped. MacVeagh informed the Greeks but in Athens they continued to believe that the 250 million credit would be given and the 25 million was the first payment. An official denial of the US Embassy did not have any effect.

MacVeagh reported angrily to Washington: *"It is most unfortunate that the question of the credit from the Export-Import Bank has been handled by the Greek Government in a manner which can only be described as careless. Greece needs almost everything that can be obtained from abroad, but there is little evidence of any sense of responsibility in arriving at a proper balance of requirements within reasonable limits of cost. Many of the requests submitted to*

UNRRA are frankly extravagant and the Eximbank list may well contain items of the same character."[1]

The Greek Government showed a similar irresponsible attitude regarding the payment of reparations from Germany. In August the State Department had asked the Greek Government to prepared a list with their demands til October. On 17 October 1945 Symeon Diamantopoulos, the Greek ambassador in Washington presented the Greek demands. They amounted to the fantastic sum of 10.449.506.903 Dollars, a number which the American Ambassador characterised as *"problematic"*,[2] when he mentioned it to Foreign Secretary Dean Acheson. At the same time the ambassador explained that the Greek government expected that foreign states would finance the reconstruction of the country. Apparently Greece relied on foreign help. In Washington they were aghast about the airy treatment of numbers.

Reparations in the Form of Benefit in Kind

In February 1945 Roosevelt, Churchill and Stalin decided that Germany should pay for the damages it had caused as far as possible. Since Germany was totally destroyed and its economy was in a sorry state it was clear that Germany could not effect any financial performance. Therefore material and monetary values in Germany and from German assets held abroad should be confiscated. Goods of the German production should be taken annually. German labour could be used for reconstruction. All this should be controlled by an Allied Reparations Commission. In the Potsdam Conference the areas in Germany were defined from which the reparation goods were to be taken: The Western Powers and the countries entitled to receive reparations were to receive their goods from Western Germany, the Soviet Union and Poland primarily from Eastern Germany.

In the Paris Reparations Agreement of 14 February 1946 it was decided that the Western reparations demand should be divided among all states entitled to receive reparations with the exception of Poland and the Soviet Union. The conference conceded to Greece 4,5 percent of the material reparations and 2,7 percent of other reparations. The money assets which were to be distributed were the foreign assets of Germany and the so-called dismantling goods, which included everything that could be disassembled. All these decisions were taken as authorized only by the Allies. The German side did not have any say, which is not astonishing since Germany was an occupied state without a government.[3] Later the distributed financial assets were estimated to have been 520 million Dollars market value of 1938. The value of the dismounted industrial plants was estimated lower. A final definition of the reparations question came on 27 February 1953 by the London Debt Agreement.[4]

During the post-war years big salvaging of industrial plants and other facilities e.g. hospitals took place in Western Germany which were transported to France and Britain as advance reparations. The US contended itself with patents and high-tech products such as rockets and jet planes. In 1948 Greece sent a commission to Western Germany which was to enforce the Greek demands. The material conceded to Greece consisted of *"30.000 Tonnen Maschinenmaterial, darunter mehrere große Walzenstraßen, eine größere Anzahl von Werk-*

1 United States, Department of State, *Foreign Relations of the United States 1945,* VIII (Washington: Government Printing Office, 1969), p. 244. Quoted as FRUS.

2 *Ibidem.* The peace treaties concluded on the Paris peace conference in 1947 provided that Italy would pay 105 million Dollars and Bulgaria 50 million Dollars to Greece. Hungary should pay 200 millions and Rumania 300 million Dollars to the Soviet Union.

3 To come to the conclusion that these demounted goods were no German reparations because the German government was not engaged is totally absurd.

4 Helmut Rumpf, "Die deutsche Frage und die Reparationen" http://www.zaoerv.de (1973).

zeugmaschinen, Kranteile, Gießerei- und Farbenfabrikeinrichtungen." In 1948 the entire material was transported from the Ruhr area to Hamburg and there it was stored on dumb barges because no halls were available due to the bombing.

In 1949 the material which had begun to corrode was put into a hall of MAN. In 1950 the first 10,000 tons were loaded on a British freighter and sent to Piraeus but it never arrived there. The remaining 18,500 tons went on corroding and blocked the MAN hall. In 1953 it became clear that the entire material had become worthless; it could only be scraped.

The Greek commissioner responsible for the reparations was a certain Georgios Lavdas who remained in Bonn when the other commissioners left Germany. As *DER SPIEGEL* wrote Lavdas was mixed up in dark business dealings in whicj other members of the embassy also participated. Lavdas spent money like water. It had been he who organized that the first transport went on an English freighter and now he arranged that the scrap was sold to a British company though a German and an Italian company which offered better prices. It can be assumed that he earned a lot in both cases. What happened to the goods on the ships is unknown. Similarly it is unknown who got the money from the sale of the scrap.

However, it became a scandal when the journalist, Vasos Mathiopoulos, of the Plastiras newspaper *Allagi* wrote about it. In the Greek embassy in Bonn they allegedly threatened him with a good bashing if did not keep his mouth shut.[1] The value of the industrial goods was at least 30 million Dollars before they corroded i.e 120 million DM at that time.

These industrial goods were excellent machines and production facilities which had been a part of the German armaments industry. In Britain these machines ran til the late 1950s as I saw with my own eyes. If these machines and production facilities had reached Greece they certainly could have formed the nucleus of a manufacturing industry. The only beneficiary was apart of the Greek oligarchy which managed to acquire the revenues of the disappeared goods.

The London Debt Agreement

In 1949 the Federal Republic of Germany came into being. In early 1950 the Cold War reached a first climax when the Korean war broke out. The Americans wanted that the FRG to rearm itself in order to strengthen the defence of Western Europe. Adenauer declared himself ready to do this but pointed out that either the FRG could rearm or pay reparations. To do both would outrun the economic power of the FRG. The Americans, however, wanted the rearmament. Now long difficult negotiations began which ended 1953 with the Londn Debt Agreement.

In the London Debt Agreement of 27 February 1953 it was decided that German reparations would be paid only when the two Germanies were re-united or by bi-lateral agreements. The German pre-war and post-war debts were not touched by this agreement. These essentially consist of the Prussian foreign loans and those of the Deutsche Reich and about the debts which came into being after the war. Their total was considered to be 15,28 billion DM. Since nobody could imagine that the two Germanies would be reunited the reparations were postponed until doomsday. Greece and Yugoslavia also signed this agreement.[2] With this agreement the FRG had a legal basis to reject all demands for reparations before the re-unification of Germany.

---

1 "Reparationen. Dein Maul zu halten" *Der Spiegel* (22. Oktober 1952).

2 Christoph Buchheim, "Das Londoner Schuldenabkommen", in: Ludolf Herbst (ed.): *Westdeutschland 1945–1955. Unterwerfung, Kontrolle, Integration* (München; Oldenbourg, 1986),pp. 219–229.

But there were two exceptional cases: Yugoslavia and Greece- When Nikita Khrushchev visited Yugoslavia in the mid-1950s the US became afraid that Yugoslavia might drift again to the eastern block In order to prevent this the US pressed Bonn to pay reparations to Yugoslavia. Bonn did this and paid 60 million DM cash to Yugoslaa and an investment credit of 240 million DM with a run time of 99 years.

Greek Efforts to Get German Economic Aid

Since 1947 the Greek politicians relied on the Americans that they would fill the Greek budget gap and would support Greece financially. McNeill described this behaviour accurately: *"Greek politicians found no real need to do more than agree in words with American demands for economy and reorganization in government. So long as the Americans were prepared to pump hundreds of millions of dollars into the economy each year, why should the Greek government not run an unbalanced budget and let the balance of foreign payments take care of itself? The Americans would have to make the deficits good; and if they complained of the use to which their funds were put, one would mollify them with promises for the future. [...] The United States owed them a great debt of gratitude for having fought the guerilla war and stopped the advance of Communism. [...] Some politicians were even inclined to feel that it would not really be a good thing to balance the budget and correct the shortfall in exports, for if these things were done, then the crying need for American aid would disappear, and the country might then be left to fend for itself economically."* [1]

However in 1953 the Eisenhower administration chose to close the chronic gap in the Greek budget and drastically curtailed the supporting payments. The American behaviour made it clear to the Greeks that from now on they could not expect substantial economic aid. In Athens it was understood that one needed other money sources and Britain and the FRG were the first candidates. In July 1953 Markezinis visited London and had talks with governmental authorities and outstanding business leaders which all were very cordial but brought no results.[2] Therefore the FRG remained the only candidate.

Markezinis visited Bonn and announced after his return that the German Government had promised to grant a credit of 200 million DM. Because Adenauer intended to visit Greece in March 1954 a credit grantor had to be found. Though the minister of finance rejected the credit the cabinet decided to entitle the *Kreditanstalt für Wiederaufbau* (credit bank for reconstruction) to give a tax privileged credit of 250 million DM.[3] Thus an unstressed visit of Adenauer in Athens on 9 March was assured.

Adenauer's visit in Greece was the first whatever of a German head of government whatsoever. The official program lasted from 10 to 12 March 1954. Adenauer made some conciliatory gestures and his daughter handed over a cheque of 50,000 DM to Queen Frederika for the reconstruction of Kalavryta. This gesture, however, was made in vain because the Queen misplaced the cheque and found it again after eight months.[4] Whether the money arrived in Kalavryta is unknown However Adenauer's voyage to Greece fulfilled with substance the agreement about economic cooperation with substance. From then on German industry was expected to contribute to the reconstruction of Greece and promote the country

1 William Hardy McNeill, *Greece: American Aid in Action 1947-1956* (New York: The Twentieth Century Fund, 1957), p. 61.

2 Spyros Linardatos, *Apo ton emfylio sti chounta,* II (Athen: Papazisis, 1977), p. 89f.

3 22nd session of the Cabinet on 8 March 1954 C. "Finanzierung Industrieller Vorhaben in Griechenland". http://www.bundesarchiv.de/cocoon/barch/0000/k/k1954k/kap1_2/kap2_9/para3_5.html

4 Ehrengard Schramm, *Ein Hilfswerk für Griechenland. Begegnungen und Erfahrungen mit Hinterbliebenen deutscher Gewalttaten der Jahre 1941-1944* (Göttingen: Vandenhoeck & Ruprecht, 2003), p. 53.

economically by investments. The Greek side promised to restore former property of the German Reich to the FRG.[1]

In June 1954 Prime Minister Papagos appeared in Bonn for a return visit. He brought with him a bill which had passed the Greek parliament just before his visit. It dealt with the restitution of former German financial assets. An agreement on economic questions was signed. In November 1954 Ludwig Erhard, Minister of economic, visited Athens. The German financial assets were restored and Erhard prolonged the term of the credit substantially and agreed that the quantity of Greek wines and tobacco was increased. One had arrived at the *quid pro quo* system i.e. in normalcy.[2]

In 1955 Karamanlis became Prime Minister. Like his predecessors he tried to receive American economic aid. But by the Eisenhower doctrine only directly threatened states received aid. During talks in Washington he reminded the relevant people that the US had always paid the deficit in the Greek budget. The Americans reacted friendly but remained noncommittal.[3] Thus it was clear that Karamanlis had to fid other money sources. He did not want credits which would increase the debt of the country but payments which would not be repaid. However with the exception of the US no other state could grant such lost benefits, let alone then the FRG.

The German-Yugoslav negotiation had been watched in Athens and when the results became known in October 1956 Athens in the person of trade minister Panagiotis Papaligouras addressed the German Embassy in Athens demanding economic aid. The minister mentioned the help which Yugoslavia had obtained. The FRG was the most important trade partner of Greece and the strongest economic force in Europe. Economic aid would fix Greece in the Western camp. Marginally Papaligouras hinted that Germany had the duty to pay reparations to Greece for the war damages. The Greek Government was thinking of a long term credit.[4] Thus the Greek side tried to imitate the Yugoslav proceeding and obtain reparations tarnished as a long term credit.

Ambassador Kordt recommended a benevolent examination of the Greek wish. The AA was against a rejection of the wish but the Ministry of Finance was against it as before in the Yugoslav case. There was no means for credits to foreign states. There should not be created another precedent. Besides that, the budgetary position was strained. The Ministry of Economics saw the case in a more differentiated manner. Greece had suufferd mor by WWII and the civil war than Yugoslavia. The Greek press attacked the Athens government because it did not demand reparations from the FRG as Yugoslavia had done. Since the Eastern Block tried to penetrate the Greek market by offering cheap goods, it would be reasonable to help the Greeks with 150-200 million DM credit and a minimum term of 10-20 years. The necessary means for this could be taken out of the budget of the developmental aid.[5]

In early March ambassador Kordt reported that the demands for reparations were vehemently discussed in the Greek parliament and the demand of German economic aid became stronger. The question of the reparations, which had not been paid, was suitable to make the feelings run high, Precisely because Greece had signed the London Debt Agreement this increased the moral pressure on Germany to grant Greece extensive economic aid.[6] When in

---

1 Olga Lazaridou, *Von der Krise zur Normalität, Die deutsch-griechischen Beziehungen unter besonderer Berücksichtigung der politischen und wirtschaftlichen Grundlagen (1949-1958)* Diss. (Bonn, 1992), p. 165.
2 Lazaridou, *op. cit.*, p. 179f.
3 *FRUS 1955-1957*, XXIV, pp. 574-576.
4 Lazaridou, *op. cit.*, p. 211f.
5 *Ibidem*, p. 213f.
6 *Ibidem*, p. 215f.

March 1957 vice-chancellor Franz Blücher visited Athens and met Karamanlis the latter spoke about the economic help. In April and May these approaches continued and the Yugoslav aid was mentioned. During the Greek-German economic discussions at the end of May Economic Minister Erhard gave to understand that Germany was principally ready to assist the Greek economic reconstruction by granting so-called Hermes monetary bonds but the granting of government bonds would be a total political *novum*. The Yugoslav bond had been granted out of political reasons and for such topics the Foreign Minister was the correct contact person. By this statement Erhard signalled that he advocated support for Greece.[1]

At the beginning of June the process of forming an opinion among the various departments of the government was roughly finished. It was agreed that Greece should be helped. The grant of a bond, however, was excluded because such a bond needed the agreement of the parliament which was difficult to obtain because elections were imminent. However the financing of long term investments should be checked. The Greek side, however, insisted and mentioned the not paid reparations for war destructions in order to put pressure on the process. In early July Bonn decided that Greece would receive a low coupon credit of 50-75 million DM.[2] Whether this change of opinion had been caused by the Greek demand of reparations is unclear but it might have played a role.

From 6 to 10 July 1957 minister of trade Papaligouras came to Bonn invited by vice-chancellor Blücher. During these talks the Greek deliveries of ammunition to Germany were one topic. Papaligouras on the other hand informed his dialogue partners in Bonn about Greek plans of developing the infra structure. Because of supply difficulties of the Greeks and changes of the armament of the German army (Bundeswehr) the ammunitions project could be realised only in a rather restricted form. Undersecretary of state, Westrick, of the ministry of economics suggested to support the electrical power plant of Ptolemaida in the lignite area by a German credit. Adenauer considered this project as the only realisable one.[3]

Papaligouras returned to Athens highly satisfied. Since Bonn, however, did nothing to keep the promise frustration in Athens was growing because it was noticed that Bonn accommodated the Yugoslavs. In November 1957 the economic talks were resumed but did not lead to any concrete result.

Reparations and the Merten Case

However in the meantime a new element had turned up in this case. Ob 26 April 195z the lawyers, Dr. Max Merten, was arrested as a war criminal in Athens.[4] Details about the Merten case are published in this book thus here only the direct connection with reparations question will be described.

Already at the end of April the German embassy wrote to the AA that the forthcoming trial of Mertan was a means to exert pressure to *"in der Frage der Entschädigung [...] zu einer Lösung zu kommen."* In Athens it was hoped that the whole affair would go off without a hitch.[5] On 15 May the embassy informed the AA that the Greek government had used all possibilities to get financial reparations. On 20 May the counsellor of the embassy Gustav von

1 *Ibidem*, p. 217f.

2 *Ibidem*, p. 218f.

3 *Ibidem*, p. 220f; 188. Cabinet session on 10 July 1957: http://www.bundesarchiv.de/cocoon/barch/0000/k/-k1957k/kap1_2/kap2_29/para3_11.html: http://www.bundesarchiv.de/cocoon/barch/0000/k/k1958k/kap1_2/kap-2_24/para3_12.html.

4 See chapter; "The War Criminal Max Merten".

5 Susanne-Sophia Spiliotis, *Der Fall Merten, Athen 1959: Ein Kriegsverbrecherprozeß im Spannungsfeld von Wiedergutmachungs- und Wirtschaftspolitik* MA-Arbeit (München, 1991), p. 64. BA/B 305-1041.

Schmoller wrote that *"Griechenland [...] durch deutsche Schuld schwer gelitten und im Krieg hohe Verluste an Menschen und Wirtschaftsgütern [hat] hinnehmen müssen."* It could be understood that the Greeks expected an equivalent if they proved themselves generous in the question of the war criminals. The Greek proposals should be checked quickly.[1]

On 20 May it was demanded in the AA that the Merten case had to separated from the question of reparations. The BMJ proposed to put pressure on Greece if Merten was not released. A representative of the AA suggested that the Greeks could be informed that the AA was thinking about a travel warning to all those who had been in Greece in WWII. Athens was angry because Yugoslavia had received 320 million DM and Turkey 740 million DM economic aid. The economic situation of Greece was so desperate that Athens was ready to use every means to obtain money. The embassy should be informed that one did not accept any link.[2]

On 23 April the AA instructed the embassy in Athens to demand the immediate release of Merten and his unhindered departure. The position of the FRG in the reparations question was known.[3] On 16 May 1957 the German embassy in Athens informed the AA that a suspension of the trial could only be expected in connection with a solution of the reparations question. The AA was advised to consider the matter benevolently.[4]

On 22 May *Der Spiegel* wrote: *"Die Lösung des Rätsels ist, dass Merten das erste Opfer einer Auseinandersetzung wurde, in deren Verlauf die griechische Regierung seit einem Jahr auf gut balkanische Weise versucht, die Bundesregierung unter Druck zu setzen und sie zu außerplanmäßigen Reparationsleistungen zu veranlassen."*[5] This article and several other similar ones caused angry reactions of the Greek Government. The embassy warned Bonn repeatedly, the AA and the BMJ, however, remained in the negative position. The Ministry of Justice was especially stubborn and arrogant because it demanded from the Greeks to stop the trial. Again Schmoller warned: *"Wird der griechische Vorschlag unter Berufung auf das Londoner Schuldenabkommen a limine abgelehnt, so werden die Prozesse mit allen geschilderten unerfreulichen Folgen und ohne Rücksicht auf die Belastung des deutsch-griechischen Verhältnisses durchgeführt werden."*[6] Bonn, however, remained with their opinion that the Greeks tried all possibilities *"um zu einer Geldentschädigung zu kommen."* This was proved at the parallel German-Greek economic negotiations.[7]

After a lot of see-saw Minister of Justice Hans-Joachim von Merkatz stated in aletter to Foreign Minister Heinrich von Brentano on 17 October 1957 that the affair could not dealt with by judicial means. The difficulties created by the Merten case could only be overcome by German-Greek negotiations about reparations. Although the reparations demands did not comply with the London Debt Agreement the only way to remove the Greek-German tensions was this solution.[8]

On 15 March 1958 the Greek government handed over a memorandum to the German Embassy in which was stated that the payng of reparations was the only solution of the war

---

1 Hagen Fleischer/Despina Konstantinakou, "Ad calendas graecas? Griechenland und die deutsche Wiedergutmachung", in: Hans Günter Hockerts et al. (Eds.), *Grenzen der Wiedergutmachung. Die Entschädigung für NS-Verfolgte in West-und Osteuropa 1945-2000* (Göttingen: Wallstein, 2006), p. 400.
2 Note for the file DBMdJ 9250/1-3-12562/57 of 20 May 1957. BA B 141/9566, pp. 37-44.
3 BA B 141/9566, p. 51.
4 RK 515-10 Ber. Nr. 533/57 vom 16. Mai 1957 BA B 141/9566, pp. 62-67.
5 "Griechenland Beziehungen. Die Falle der Fahndung" *Der Spiegel* 21 (22. Mai 1957), p. 15.
6 Spiliotis, *op. cit.*, p. 69.
7 *Ibidem*, p. 71.
8 *Ibidem*, p. 71.

criminals problem. Though the German negative attitude was known the memo assured a continuous cooperation. The government did not have ny influence on the Greek justice. If Merten was condemned he would be amnestied speedily. In the AA they tried to get Merten free without any concessions. Perhaps Federal President Heuss could appeal to King Paul. On the Greek side also there were efforts to solve the problem quietly. But all these efforts led nowhere because at the end of March the chamber responsible for war criminals decided to transfer the Merten case to a special military court.

In Bonn the AA had brought itself to submit a new offer to the Greeks: If the Greeks assured that Merten would be released sooner or later an economic delegation may come to Bonn to negotiate about economic aid. With this it was clear that Bonn had accepted a link between the Merten trial and economic aid. *"Die von griechischer Seite angestrebte deutsche Wirtschaftshilfe verstärkt unsere Position. Die deutsche Botschaft wird beim Außenminister in Griechenland vorsichtig durchblicken lassen, dass es in der deutschen Öffentlichkeit nicht verstanden würde, wenn solche Verhandlungen vor der Regelung des Falles Merten stattfänden."*[1] These hints were probably made because a little later the Greek Government announced the release of a special law for war criminals. It was a signal snt to Bonn: New negotiations should start before the bilateral relation were further damaged by the Merten case. However this did not hinder the Greek Government from examining German tourist by the police whether or not they had committed war crimes in Greece.[2]

In early September the economic negotiations began which were constantly strained by the Merten case. Both sides agreed that economic help was a suitable means to forget the remembrance of the past. Bonn gave to understand that the Merten case might impair the granting of economic aid especially as there was the danger that the parliament (Bundestag) would not agree if the Merten case was brought to an end. The Greek side promised to find a solution for this problem before the signing of the economic agreement.[3]

On 10 November 1958 Karamanlis arrived in Bonn. The legal department of the AA had suggested that Adenauer should hint during his conversation with Karamanlis that *"die Bundesregierung selbstverständlich mit der Zusage rechne, dass die griechische Regierung die Kriegsverbrecher-Frage klären, bzw. den verhafteten Merten überstellen werde."* If the war criminals problem was not solved before the agreement was ratified the Bundestag might make trouble.[4]

Karamanlis promised to release a special law which would enable the deportation of Merten.[5] However he could not keep his promise because of the public excitement. The main weight of the negotiations between Karamanlis and the Bonn government was on the economic sector.

The *Neue Zürcher Zeitung* commented the outcome descriptively: *"Der Fischzug des griechischen Ministerpräsidenten in Bonn hat sich gelohnt. Im Netz blieben zwar keine politisch unmittelbar zu verwertenden Formulierungen zur Cypernfrage hängen, dafür aber ein ansehnlicher Klumpen Rheingold."*[6] Indeed with the exception of Yugoslavia the Bonn Government had not granted such a consolidated bond to any other state. The sum of 200 million DM was considerable. Besides the results mentioned before there were others which were also

---

1 AA (Ref. 503) - Note of 22 May 1958: BA/B 305-1047. Quoted from Spiliotis, *op. cit.*, p. 103.

2 BdBRD - SE - 204 Merten Ber. No. 608/58 vom 14. Juni 1958: BA B141/9568, p. 13f.

3 *Ibidem*, p. 119.

4 Lazaridou, *op. cit.*, p. 257.

5 Spiliotis, *op. cit.*, p. 120.

6 *Neue Zürcher Zeitung* (14. November 1958) Quoted from. Lazaridou, *op. cit.*, p. 241.

important The bond strengthened Karamanlis' position against the opposition led by EDA which had been invigorated in the 11 May 1958 elections. The economic advancement of Greece would be promoted by the link with the FRG. And finally the credit was useful for the German industry because the investment goods would be delivered from German firms. However then such thoughts were usual in all cases of development aid. As a quid pro quo Karamanlis had promised to end the question of the war criminals, i.e. to solve the Merten case. As we have already seen Karamanlis could keep this promise only in a limited way.

In December 1990 the newspaper *To Vima* published the secret report of the economic scientist Angelos Angelopoulos of 26 September 1964 which he had sent to the then foreign Minister of Greece, Stavros Kostopoulos. In this report it became clear that the negotiations had included another topic as well. In his report Angelopoulos wrote that in a conversation with the two ministerial directors Ernst Féaux de la Croix und Hermann Reinhardt of the ministries of finance and economy the latter had said that Karamanlis, during the negotiations in November 1958 in order to get the 200 million credit had renounced the back payment of the so-called occupation loan (katochiko daneio). But there existed no written waiver declaration.[1] Thus this topic remained alive until now. We will come back to it later in this book.

How much Bonn sought to help Greece was seen when the offer of the ammunition delivery was presented. Though the Greek offer was 6,3 million DM higher than the cheapest offer from another European state and the General Accounting Office criticised, out of political reasons it it was decided to give the order to Greece and book the difference as economic aid for Greece.[2]

Thus Greece received 200 million DM reparations tarnished as an investment credit. With this money Greece was electrified. Til then only the big towns had had electricity. The power plant of Ptolemaida, the overhead power lines, the transformers and so on were paid for with this money. The average Greek did not understand what was going on, however the members of the electricity company (DEI) did so. My friend Kostas Sarropoulos who had studied engineering in Germany told me many years ago that the construction of the electricity net was a reparations benefit. In the eyes of many Greek politicians these items were no reparations because German companies earned money by it. It was not noted that the financing had been made by German tax money and that Greece did not have to pay anything The main underlying thought, however, was that the politicians could not divert parts of the money. Electric installations could nott be diverted into the pockets of the politicians as cash money.

Reparations of Italy and Bulgaria

At this point it seems reasonable to have a look at the reparations payments of the other two occupation powers (Italy and Bulgaria). The Italian reparations had been fixed at 105 million Dollars in the peace treaty of 1947 between Greece and Italy. A little later it was reduced to 100,8 million Dollars. In 1961 the American Embassy in Athens stated that Italy had paid in the form of old ships and power plant equipment so that only 15 million Dollars remained. However the prices of these goods had been much higher than those on the world market. In 1953 a reparations agreement was concluded by which 4,8 million Dollars were paid to 3.000 Greeks.

1 Lazaridou, *op. cit.*, p. 244f. D. Nikolakopoulos, "Zitame apo ti nea Germania na epistrepsei ta ... daneika" To Vima (16. Dezember 1990).

2 53rd Cabinet Session on 4 February 1959: http://www.bundesarchiv.de/cocoon/barch/0111/k/k1959k/kap1_2/-kap2_5/para3_2.html.

At the peace conference Greece had demanded from Bulgaria 985 million Dollars reparations but only 45 million Dollars had been ascribed to Greece. Bulgaria refused to pay and demanded an accounting with Greek debts of the pre-war time. In 1965 finally Sofia agreed to pay 7 million Dollars in the form of goods to be delivered.[1]

Negotiations About Compensations

In summer 1956 eleven Western European states jointly asked the FRG government to pay compensation for false imprisonment of persecuted persons of the Nazis (i.e. not for forced labourers or resistance fighters). In December 1958 Bonn informed these countries that the FRG war ready to negotiate about this. However the provisions of the London Debt Agreement must not be violated and the financial abilities of the FRG must not be overstrained. It was stressed that they payments were voluntary.[2]

On 8 December 1958 the German government signalled Greece in a diplomatic note that it was ready to start negotiations about compensations.[3] The topics of these negotiations were not reparations and war crimes as in the negotiations in November 1956 but the compensation of crimes out of racist motives the so-called global agreement (Globalabkommen).[4]

On 18 February 1959 the law of the suspension of the criminal prosecution of war criminals entered into force. However the word amnesty was not included. On 5 March 1959 Merten was sentenced to 25 years in Prison. Though the Greek Government had promised to release Merten soon after the judgement in May 1959 he was still in prison though ambassador Seelos had intervened with Karamanlis several times. Ambassador Ypsilantis gave to understand that they were waiting for a suitable moment then the release could be managed without great excitement of the public.[5] However it is quite possible that Merten was kept in prison to be able to exert pressure during the negotiations about the compensations which were beginning.[6]

Before the first negotiations round in May 1959 Bonn asked the eight governments for precise numbers of their demands. At the same time the German embassies in thee countries were ordered to start researches. The numbers which Greece submitted appeared the AA too high and too unspecified when they compared them with publicly accessible data. During the first round of the negotiations from 4 to 6 May the Greek side tried to push through a maximum demand of compensations for 190.800 former persecuted persons. It was obvious that this number included resistance fighters and other persons for which there would be no compensations. While Athens tried to push the number as high as possible Bonn tried to lower it. That was the about 10,000 Jews that had survived the war who had the right to ask for compensations for racial persecution. In Greece nobody had lost his life for religious reasons. Ideological reasons referred to the communists but most of them had lost their lives because of resistance actions.[7]

---

1 Hagen Fleischer/Despina Konstantinakou, "Ad calendas graecas?", p. 386; *FRUS 1958-1960*, X, 2, p. 690 Fußnote 2. *Keesing's Contemporary Archives*, p. 20.198.

2 Hagen Fleischer/Despina Konstantinakou, "Ad calendas graecas", pp. 375-457.

3 Spiliotis, *op. cit.*, p. 149.

4 "Globalentschädigungsabkommen: Verteilung an *„zugunsten der aus Gründen der Rasse, des Glaubens oder der Weltanschauung von nationalsozialistischen Verfolgungsmaßnahmen betroffenen Staatsangehörigen, die durch diese Verfolgungsmaßnahmen Freiheitsschäden oder Gesundheitsschädigungen erlitten haben, sowie besonders auch zugunsten der Hinterbliebenen der infolge dieser Verfolgungsmaßnahmen Umgekommenen.*" http://www.-auswaertiges-amt.de/DE/Aussenpolitik/InternatRecht/Entschaedigung_node.html

5 Spiliotis, *op. cit.*, p. 138.

6 *Ibidem*, p. 140.

7 Fleischer, *Calendas*, pp. 402-405.

Thus the first negotiation round brought no result. The different opinions about the groups which might get a compensation intensified. Therefore the German side demanded a list of the persecuted with details about the reasons of the detention and its length in order to calculate the entitlements. The negotiations should be interrupted til the list was submitted.[1]

On 17 October 1959 the Greek government submitted a draft law to rump parliament by which all German war criminal cases should be definitely suspended without any exception. The opposition criticised this as a violation of the constitution. A rump parliament could not release such a bill which was relevant for internal and external policy. It demanded that this bill was discussed by the full parliament. Because this would have meant publicity and excitement the ERE majority of the rump parliament rejected it. The bill provided an immediate stop of all cases against war criminals and their persecution and the release of all imprisoned and their deportation. The latter concerned Merten. Additionally the national war criminal office was to be dissolved.[2] As in the law of 18 February 1959 the word amnesty was missing. The opposition accused the government of colluding with the Germans. When criticism in the ERE-party began foreign minister Averof also told the deputies that the negotiation about the compensation agreement was running very well. [3]

During the violent parliamentary debate of the compensation bill it became clear that it was closely linked with the repartions payment and the release of Merten. On 23 October 1959 the bill passed with majority of the ERE votes. On 3 October it became a law. On 5 October Merten was deported to Germany. On 30 October ambassador Seelos admonished Bonn: *"Eine baldige positive Regelung der Frage der Entschädigung von Naziopfern, ist daher jetzt von akuter Bedeutung, wenn die mit dem Gesetz zur Beendigung der Kriegsverbrecherfrage von beiden Seiten angestrebte psychologische Wirkung nicht in ihr Gegenteil umschlagen soll."*[4]

The Global Agreement

The German embassy in Athens worriedly observed the inner Greek discussion which became more and more heated and advised the AA to compensate also the victims of sanctions: *"Die psychologische Wirkung unserer freiwilligen Zahlung [würde] stark beeinträchtigt [...], wenn Ortschaften wie Kalavryta und Distomon überhaupt nicht berücksichtigt werden. Im übrigen dürfte es sich bei den zum Teil barbarischen mit keinem Kriegsrecht zu vereinbarenden Metzeleien, die deutsche SS-Einheiten unter den unschuldigen Bewohnern zahlreicher griechischer Ortschaften veranstaltet haben, in deren Nähe Partisanentätigkeit beobachtet worden war, doch tatsächlich um ausgesprochen nationalsozialistisches Unrecht handeln und dürften wir jedes Interesse daran haben, dass diese Maßnahmen als solche angesehen werden."*[5]

At the same time the Greek side made an effort to get a free hand in the distribution of the money received. Averof warned otherwise the money would go to the Jews and the Communists. Seelos was skeptical about this demand. He considered the method practised in other countries to keep away from the distribution of the money as wrong in Greece. If Germany did not have a say in distribution of the money it might *"allzusehr für eigene politische Zwecke missbraucht werden."*[6]

1 Spiliotis, *op. cit.*, p. 138.
2 Spiliotis, *op. cit.*, p. 141.
3 Spiliotis, *op. cit.*, p. 141.
4 Spiliotis, *op. cit.*, p. 143f.
5 Fleischer, *Calendas*, p. 413f. Kalavryta was a crime committed by the Wehrmacht. Meyer, *op. cit.*, *passim*.
6 Fleischer, *Calendas*, p. 413.

In the AA voices were heard which were in favour of compensating the victims of the mass retaliation actions such as Kalvryta and Distomon because these had not been military measures but measures based on the Nazi ideology. However those responsible saw this differently. Hints were made to Athens in January 1960 that the negotiations of Greece about an association with the EWG (European Economic Community) should not be burdened with excessive compensation demands.[1]

The ministry of finance considered the Greek demands as exaggerated. Til the end of 1958 the Federal Government had believed that 100 million DM would be sufficient to satisfy the demands of all Western states. However alone the Greek demand alone was double as high than that. The ministry of finance estimated the realistic Greek demands to be 65 million DM and was against the polititical considerations of the AA ro show themselves generous to the Greeks. In February 1960 the undersecretary of the AA, Albert van Scherpenberg, urged the ministry of finance: He considered it necessary to make on offer to the Greek government which it could present to the parliament and the opposition. One should not frustrate the Greek public. The negotiations should be speeded up.[2]

In mid-February 1960 the next round of negotiations took place. The Greek side rejected the 60 million DM offered as much too low. The Greek public had expected 200 million DM but would be satisfied with a sum between 130 and 150 million DM. Foreign minister von Brentano had allegedly mentioned 120 million DM to Averof. Only such a sum could take the wind out of the opposition's sails. The representative of the ministry of finance tried to block this by stating that he did not know this. Scherpenberg, however, understood that action was needed and turned to his colleague of the BMF, Karl Hettlage, He told him the negative consequences of a low offer. Karamanlis should not loose his face when he mentioned the number in parliament. Also the German embassy in Athens warned against a sum much lower than 120 million DM. This would trigger a huge hate campaign. But the BMF continued to block. The did not want to surpass the sum of 65 million DM.[3]

Finally ambassador Ypsilantis asked for a meeting with Adenauer. It is not known what was said during this meeting but after the end of it the chancellor called together a special meeting of the cabinet. The AA and the BMF prepared statements. During the meeting on 2 March mainly Adenauer, Brentano and Hettlage spoke. Since the minister of finance did not support Hettlage he fought his last stand but then Adenauer intervened. The cabinet decided that the negotiations with the Greeks should continue on the basis of 100 million. Should the Greeks demand more then the maximum would be 115 million DM.[4]

Now a new poker round began. The Greek side insisted on 120 million. On the following day the German side slowly increased the sum but offering resistance. Finally on 9 March 1960 the sum of 115 million DM was agreed upon which would be paid in four parts. On 18 March the German-Greek Global Agreement was signed. This in four days the sum had been doubled. During the negotiations of the global agreement with the other Western states such a thing did not happen. It was a unique case.[5]

Article 1 of the agreement read that Germany paid Greece 155 million DM *"zugunsten der aus Gründen der Rasse, des Glaubens oder der Weltanschauung von nationalsozialistischen Verfolgungsmaßnahmen betroffenen griechischen Staatsangehörigen. Die Verteilung des Betrages bleibt dem Ermessen der Königlichen Griechischen Regierung überlassen."* Article 2

---

1 *Ibidem*, p. 414.
2 Spiliotis, *op. cit.*, p. 147.
3 Fleischer, *Calendas*, p. 417f.
4 *Ibidem*, p. 418f.
5 *Ibidem*, p. 419f.

stated that the sum would be paid in four rates. The last rate would be paid on 1 March 1963. Article 3 stated clearly that with this payment *"alle den Gegenstand dieses Vertrages bildenden Fragen im Verhältnis der Bundesrepublik Deutschland zu dem Königreich Griechenland [...are] abschließend geregelt"* At the end of the text it was stated that the agreement did not need any ratification. In an accompanying text it was stated that the Bonn government acted on the assumption that the Greek government would *"künftig an sie mit dem Verlangen nach Regelung weiterer Fragen, die aus nationalsozialistischen Verfolgungsmaßnahmen während Kriegs- und Besatzungszeit herrührten, nicht herantreten wird."* In his reply ambassador Ypsilantis agreed in the name of his government but precluded the right that if according to the London Debt Agreement the two Germanies were re-united new demands of reparations could be raised.[1] In view of the then existing situation the question of reparations was closed for ever. A reunification of the two inimical Germanies was considered imposible.

When the negotiations of the Global Agreement were on the homestretch Merten could be released without a risk. Merten was the bargaining chip in both negotiations. Spiliotoos is right when she wrote: Merten *"war das Faustpfand der Griechen für ihre Option auf Entschädigungszahlungen."*[2]

The Distribution of the 115 Million DM

According to the ideas of the Bonn government the means of the Global Compensation were primarily to be distributed among the racial persecuted persons. But it had been accepted that also victims of hostage executions and massacres of the Wehrmacht and the SS should be compensated. Like in all other global agreements the German government had agreed that the distribution should be made by the relevant governments. This functioned well in all Western European countries and the means were distributed in a just manner in Greece, however, this was different because of the clientelistic system. Right from the beginning it had been clear that persons who had claims and were close to ERE would be preferred.[3] Besides that the Jews would not be indemnified to the degree it could be expected because they were still citizens of second class. Jews who were close to EDA would not even remain empty handed. They were not even informed about the possibilities as I was informed by leftist Jews in Thessaloniki in 1991.

During the negotiations of the Global Compensation the representative of the Central Council of Jews, Constant, had several times suggested *"in den Vertrag eine Bestimmung aufzunehmen, die die für die rassisch Verfolgten in Betracht kommende Summe ausweist und der griechischen Regierung die Auflage zu machen, diese Summe auch für die überlebenden Juden Griechenlands zu verwenden."*[4] Constant knew that the entitlement of many Jew to a payment of compensation was dubious. The BMJ saw this also. In an internal expertise they came to the conclusion that many of the as "allogenes" were not entitled at all. However the 4,000 surviving Jews were entitled to 10,8 million DM, i.e. 150 DM per month for 18 months. The BMJ emphasized to Constant that the 115 million DM were exclusively for the Jews. Since Constant did not succeed to add the proposed clause the Greek government could extend

1 *Bundesgesetzblatt* (1961) II, p. 1597f.

2 Spiliots, *op. cit.*, p. 155.

3 Fleischer, *Calendas*, p. 428. *"Die Opposition befürchtete nicht nur eine Kungelei der regierungsparteilich verfilzten Administration zugunsten von Antragstellern mit 'rechter' Gesinnung, sondern auch Abzweigungen für obskure Entwicklungsprojekte."*

4 Spiliotis, *op. cit.*, p. 150f.

the compensation to other groups as well. Therefore the Greek Jews received only 59 percent of the money granted to them by courts.[1]

However not only were the Jews cheated but also the Greek victims of German retaliatory measures. Originally 35,000 Drachmae should be paid for each violent death (1 DM = 7,5 Drachmae).[2] In the case of Kalavryta 32,000 Drachmae were paid which was a considerable sum because a teacher earned 1,100 Drachmae per month. At the end each family received 17,000 Drachmae though in many cases more than one male family member had been killed. More was promised but nothing came any more. The distribution of the money was carried out by the government according the principle of clientelism i.e only the members of the government's party were supported. Villages in which the EDA had obtained the majority of the votes at the last election received nothing.[3] In Distomon the families of victims came better off because the families received a compensation for each family member killed. The data of the total sum stretched from 8,000 to 39,000 Drachmae. For each victim 8-10,000 Drachmae were paid.[4]

A former member of the German embassy in Athens told me some years ago that only the first rate was distributed by the Greek government, i.e. 35 million DM. The justification was incredible: There were too many claims for compensation. Allegedly large parts were used to close the chronic holes in the budget. In a letter to me he wrote: *"Näheres über die Verteilung der 115 Mio. ist mir nicht bekannt, es gingen damals Gerüchte um, dass die Politiker untereinander zankten, denn jeder wollte den größten Teil für seinen eigenen Wahlbezirk in Anspruch nehmen. Immer die gleiche 'Story'. Diese Gerüchte kursierten damals auch in der Botschaft."*[5]

German Reunification

The London Debt Agreement was in force until the sudden totally unexpected reunification of Germany. Yugoslavia and Greece were the only states that had received reparations. Had a peace treaty been concluded the problem of reparations would have surfaced again. But as the bad consequences of the peace treaty of Versailles were remembered all states involved agreed that such a case must never occur again. Therefore the Two-Plus-Four Treaty as ersatz which excluded a repetition of the negative consequences of the Versailles treaty. In an additional protocol all European states disclaimed reparations. Though not all states signed this protocol but not one state entered a written objection. According to diplomatic usus an abstention or a non-agreement without a written declaration is an approval. Greece, indeed, did not sign the protocol but did not file an objection in written form. Thus it agreed de facto and de jure.

All Greek governments knew this with the exception of the first Tsipras government which knew none of the demanded reparations. Tsipras seemed not to have been informed when he raised his first claim for reparations. He demanded reparations of 273 billions Euros. Apparently he did not understand that there is no judicial way to a new debate on reparations.

1 *Ibidem*, pp. 150-152.
2 Fleischer, *Calendas*, p. 429.
3 Meyer, *Kalavryta*, p. 484.
4 These informations obtained Brigitte Spuller from citizens of Distomon. Frau Spuller organized from 1986 tils 2012 the regularly taking place meetings of the youth of the evangelische Kirche in Nürnberg and Distomon. 1990 the towns of Distomon made her an honorary citizen. Frau Spuller was decorated for her reconciliation work with the Bundesverdienstkreuz. In the meantime she is attacked - without any reason.
5 Letter to me on 23 June 2016.

The Gree public and many politicians in Greece are badly or not at all informed about the real situation. Almost nobody has ever heard of the misappropriation of the salvaged industrial goods in the early 1950s. The reparations tarnished as an investment credit of 200 million DM are similarly unknown. The Global Agreement is not recognized as a reparation and it is believed that Greece still has legal claims for reparations. When the financial debt crisis broke out these demands came to the boil.

The Debt Crisis

When the debt crisis broke out clever Greek politicians developed the idea to make Germany pay the debts by reparations. Since the sums, demanded earlier, did not have the actual height they invented a back payment date from which interest was charged. The over 90 years old national hero of Greece Manolis Glezos took over the task to push the Greeks demands through. In May 1941 Glezos and his student fellow Apostolos Santas had torn down the German war standard (Reichskriegsflagge) from the Acropolis. Now he is Euro-deputy of SYRIZA. According to his calculations the alleged debts amounted to 362 billions Euros. This number includes debts from WWI. How these came into being he does not tell. Greece was neither attacked nor occupied by German troops in WWI.

On meetings organized by DIE LINKE (THE LEFT) in Germany Glezos presented this demand and appealed to those present to put pressure on the German government. He met political die-hards of the GDR and old West-German Maoists (KBW) who agreed with him. But neither Glezos nor his German comrades took notice of the fact that Germany paid reparations. The sum of 315 million DM was an enormous amount of money in the 1950s. The sum demanded by Glezos now corresponds with a one year budget of the FRG.

In the meantime a Greek parliamentary commission put together a report in which 279 billion Euros are demanded. It contains 9 billions Euros of WWI. Constantly it has been tried to make Germany pay. However the German government is meanwhile informed about the real status and rejects in a friendly way Greek demands each time.

The Greek debts will probably be paid by the European tax payers because Greece will not be able to repay them.

THE OCCUPATION LOAN

The Compulsory Loan

In July 2016 a committee of the Greek parliament submitted a report on the reparations claim of billions of Euros from Berlin. 279 billion Euros were demanded. The so-called compulsory loan (κατοχικό δάνειο) was included and its repayment was demanded. In Greece it is believed that Hitler borrowed money from Greece to finance his war with resort to violence. And this sum must be repaid. In September the parliament was to discuss this and then the government Tsipras should demand this money back.

How little German journalists are informed is shown by an article published in the *Berliner Zeitung* of February 2015 which contained this sentence: *"Im Kern geht es um eine Zwangsanleihe, die Deutschland dem besetzten Griechenland 1942 abgepresst und trotz schriftlicher Zusage nie zurückgezahlt hat."*[1] The party *Die Linke* reacted on this statement by one deputy saying that the "dodging" of the federal government and the "pushing aside of justified demands" mus have an end.[2]

However, already the word "compulsory loan" or "occupation loan" is misleading. In Greece it is believed that Germany took a loan from Greece to finance the war and also in Germany it is not clear what the term means.

The Facts

For many years serious scholarly literature has agreed that Greece cannot expect any reparation payments or can raise such demands. But in the same literature one reads that the questions of the compulsory loan or occupation loan is open. The basis of this demand is the final report of the Reichsbank of 12 April 1945.[3] There one reads on page 114: *"Demzufolge würde sich die Restschuld, die das Reich gegenüber Griechenland hat, noch auf 476 Mio. RM belaufen."* This number became the basis of all later calculations which stretch from 3 billion Euros to 11 billion Euros. The last number stems from the magazine *Focus*.[4] Extreme Greek demands speak of 1even 575 billion Euros which Germany owed to Greece, the latter numbers include reparations. With this amount the present Greek debts could be discharged.

But this sentence is not the only one in the report of the Reichsbank. In the original report it is followed by this table:

Gesamtsumme der der Deutschen Wehrmacht zur Verfügung gestellten Beträge	*786,5 Mio. RM*
Griechische Abschlagszahlungen auf Besatzungskosten	*218,5 Mio. RM*
Deutsche Anlastungen	*568,0 Mio. RM*
Deutsche Rückzahlungen	*92,0 Mio. RM*
Deutsche Restschuld	*476,0 Mio. RM*

1 Holger Schmale, "Deutsche Besatzung in Griechenland. Tsipras präsentiert eine offene Rechnung" *Berliner Zeitung* (2. Februar 2015).

2 *Ibidem*

3 Politisches Archiv des Auswärtigen Amts R 27320, p. 114.

4 "Schuldenkrise paradox Deutschland schuldet Athen elf Milliarden aus Zwangskredit" *Focus* (12. Januar 2015). http://www.focus.de/finanzen/news/staatsverschuldung/presse-deutschland-schuldet-athen-elf-milliarden-aus-zwangsanleihe_id_4397229.html

This table clearly shows that the 476 million RM were not a credit or a loan but an invoice amount regarding the occupation cost of the Greek side. That there might be an analog list showing the Greek debts to Germany has been overseen or perhaps deliberately embezzled. On page 156 of the Reichsbank report one clearly reads, "*dass das Reich durch Lebensmittellieferungen aus seinem eigenen Versorgungsraum, durch den Export von deutschen Waren, die z.T. im Reich Mangelgüter waren, und durch Zurverfügungstellung von aus den beschränkten Eigenbeständen sein Möglichstes getan hat, die Lage in Griechenland zu erleichtern.*"[1]

Even more astonishing is that the concrete reference printed on page 33 of the report, which refers clearly to a passive balance of accounts, was not noticed. There one reads: "*Bei Abschluss des deutsch-griechischen Verrechnungsverkehrs nach Räumung Griechenlands dürfte der griechische Passivsaldo [...] den Betrag von 300 Mio RM erreicht haben.*"[2]

The report of the Reichsbank is a drawing up of a balance sheet, a comparison of demands and benefits of both sides, which shows that the Greek side had debts. Since this topic is of greatest charge the development which led to it, will be described now.

The first great problem of the occupation was the famine which has been described earlier. The second was the inflation.

The Inflation

Shortly after the beginning of the war with Italy the Drachmae became inflationary. The notes in circulation raised from 6 billion at the beginning of te war to 13 billions at the beginning of the occupation. At the end of October 1942 it rose to 180 billions and was hurrying towards the trillion. One Oka olive oil (1,300 Gr) costed 30,000 Drachmae and the value of one British Pound had risen to 300,000 Drachmae. The stopped wages of the workers or little employees was 30,000 Drachmae. The attempt of the government Tsolakoglou to stop the prices by threatening massive punishment and to fight the black market not only failed but caused the opposite. The only economic institution which ran on highest tours was the bank note printers. The black marketeers and the speculators earned fortunes.

The inflation was further heated because according to the Hague Convention Greece had to pay the maintenance costs of the occupation army. Since the Greek economy and trade stagnated the state had almost no tax revenues. In order to be able to pay the maintenance cost of the occupation army the note printer rotated in highspeed which in turn increased the inflation and provoked higher demands of the occupiers which in turn increased the speed of the note printer.

In the beginning of the occupation this circulus vitiosus was increased by the occupation money. The German troops paid with "Reichskreditkassenscheinen" (RKK = notes of the Reich's credit cash office) and the Italian with notes of the Cassa Mediteranea di Credito which were made out in Mediterranean Drachmae. The RKK exchange was 1 RM to 60 Drachmae, the Italian exchange was 1 Lira to 8 Drachmae. This occupation money circulated until the end of July 1941. The German state spent 77 million RM (=4,62 billion Drachmae), the Italians spent 5 billion Mediterranean Drachmae.[3]

In March 1942 a first effort was made to get the occupation cost under control. Finance minister Sotirios Gotzamanis had protested several times to the Italian and German authorities

1 Politisches Archiv des Auswärtigen Amts R 27320, p. 156.

2 *Ibidem*, p. 33.

3 Politisches Archiv des Auswärtigen Amts R 27320, p. 79. Some years ago 57 sacks of these bills were found m the safe of the Bank of Greece, which led to a big media freak-out. *Griechenland Zeitung* (12. April 2012).

against the excessive occupation cost. Now he went to Rome to get a contractual regulation. He suggested a separation of the cost by creating two accounts. From the first account the occupation forces would receive the regular occupation costs according to the Hague Convention. These were fixed at 1,500 million Drachmae monthly for both occupants. All other costs of the occupation armies should become advance payments in the form of a forced loan taken from the other account. This was the occupation loan (κατοχικό δάνειο) an expression which is still used today. These advance payments would be compensated by the delivery of goods or would be paid back in cash. Rome agreed and the so-called "Rome agreement" was put in force at once. [1]

This would have been a reasonable agreement if the Drachmae had been stable, but by the inflation the nominal value of the advance payments rose by a factor of three. In March the advance payment had been 6,720 millions, until August it rose to 22,600 millions. In March 5.420 millions were paid to the Germans and 1.300 million to the Italians. In August these numbers were 17.850 millions and 4.750 millions respectively These payments could only be made by the rotation of the note printer which speeded up the inflation and led to further higher advance payments.[2]

In summer 1942 the situation in Greece was no situation at all as the 'Sonderbeauftragte des Reiches für wirtschaftliche und finanzielle Fragen in Griechenland' (special envoy of the Reich for economic and financial questions in Greece) wrote drastically.[3] Food could only be bought on the black market and the inflation made the price rise and the occupation costs speeded up the inflation. On 30 August 1942 ambassador Pellegrino Ghigi sent an SOS from Greece as foreign minister Ciano wrote in his diary.[4] In September a delegation of higher civil servants of the Greek economic ministry and the Bank of Greece went to Berlin led by Gotzamanis.[5] Probably in connection with this visit the specialist for economic questions of the AA, Carl Clodius, appeared in Rome to negotiate with the Italians about the financial situation of Greece. Ghigi spoke about the heavy inflation. Clodius promised to discuss this problem with his superiors after his return to Berlin.[6] After the end of their talks in Berlin the Greek delegation travelled to Rome.

On 8 October Mussolini appeared alarmed about the German attitude regarding Greece. Probably on this day Gotzamanis appeared in Rome. Clodius informed Ciano that Germany was ready to reduce its occupation costs from 18 to 15 billion Drachmae. Gotzamanis, however, considered this still too high and rejected this. On 10 October Gotzamanis declared that if it went on like it did, Greece would financially collapse in two months. On 17 October foreign minister Ribbentrop informed his Italian colleague that Neubacher would come to Rome with new proposals. Ciano decided that the banker Alberto d'Agostino should cooperate with Neubacher.[7]

At about the same time Neubacher visited the AA and had a conversation with ambassador Karl Ritter about the situation in Greece. During the conversation he developed rather unorthodox ideas: A wartime economical solution like in Germany was excluded. The supply

1 Heinz A. Richter (ed.), *Griechenland 1942-1943. Erinnerungen von Elisabeth und Konstantinos Logothetopoulos* (Ruhpolding: Rutzen, 2015), p. 16; Politisches Archiv des Auswärtigen Amts R 27320, pp. 81, 175.

2 *Ibidem*,

3 Hermann Neubacher, *Sonderauftrag Südost 1940-1945. Bericht eines fliegenden Diplomaten* (Seeheim: Buchkreis, 1966), p. 75.

4 Galeazzo Ciano, *Diario 1937-1943* (Milano: Rizzoli, 1994), p. 446.

5 Richter, *Logothetopoulos*, p. 27.

6 Ciano, *op. cit*, p. 653.

7 *Ibidem,* pp. 654-658.

of the occupations forces had to be reduced to a minimum and the supply from the mother countries had to be increased. The black market must be fought by the delivery of food and goods and by financial measures. The prices for food and goods should set free. In the AA they were impressed by Neubacher's idea and appointed him "Sonderbeauftragter des Reichs für wirtschaftliche und finanzielle Fragen in Griechenland." The economic minister, Funk, and financial minister v. Schwerin-Krosigk agreed also.

On 19 October 1942 Neubacher arrived in Rome. On 21 October ambassador Mackensen, Neubacher, d'Agostino, Ghigi and Gotzamanis met in the office of Ciano. Neubacher presented his ideas: Ciano and Gotzamanis had reservations, d'Agostino thought that they could be realized. Neubacher wrote: *"Ich einigte mich mit meinem Kollegen d'Agostino auf die denkbar verruchteste Ketzerei: die Herstellung eines freien Marktes in Griechenland."*[1]

The Miracle of October 1942

Neubacher called the events in October 1942 the "Wunder of October"; they were aided by two happenings: The first food deliveries of the international help action of the Red Cross arrived and Rommel suffered a defeat at El Alamein. The latter led to a drop of the price because the speculators believed in a near end of the war. Both factors led to a drop of food prices on the black market.

When Neubacher arrived in Athens he announced a special economic action. Already this announcement led the speculators and stopped the prices in the black market which had risen far above the normal price. And now he dealt a heavy blow to the speculators by financial means.

"1) Eine plötzliche Auszahlungssperre für die Lieferantenguthaben bei den beiden Besatzungsarmeen. Den Lieferanten wurde bedeutet, dass die laufenden Lieferungen weiter bezahlt werden, die im Augenblicke aufgelaufenen Verbindlichkeiten aber nur ratenweise bis Jahresende abgetragen werden können; infolge einer nicht näher bekannten Währungsaktion der beiden Sonderbeauftragten sei eine empfindliche Drachmenknappheit entstanden. Dieselbe Zahlungssperre wurde über die öffentlichen Kassen verhängt. Die Aufregung war gewaltig. Lieferanten liefen zu den Banken, um sich Kredite zu besorgen, dort stießen sie auf folgenden Schrecken:

2) Vollkommene Sperrung der Bankkredite für Handelsunternehmungen und Private. Industriekredite liefen weiter, aber über ein Zensorenkomitee. Das Unglück war aber noch nicht voll:

3) Die Banken wurden angewiesen, auf breiter Front mit Kreditkündigungen vorzugehen, die von der Spekulation angesichts des Zahlungsstops nur durch Verkauf der spekulativ angelegten Warenvorräte honoriert werden konnten.

4) Die Wiederherstellung des normalen Überbringerschecks, der aus steuertechnischen Gründen einer langwierigen Prozedur unterworfen war, ließ sofort das Disagio des Schecks gegenüber der Barzahlung (über 20%, die natürlich auf die Preise abgewälzt wurden) verschwinden. Ich erinnere mich noch der Freude des Bankiers d'Agostino über diese erfolgreiche Wiederherstellung des normalen Schecks. Es war seine Idee.

5) Alle Höchstpreise wurden aufgehoben."[2]

Additionally Neubacher saw to it that larger amounts of food were delivered from Germany and other states, especially from southeastern Europe (Banat). Until early 1943 65.000

---

1 Neubacher, *op. cit.*, p. 76.
2 *Ibidem*, p. 78.

t wheat, 50.000 t legumes and 40.000 t sugar were imported.[1] Neubacher had heard that great stocks of olive oil, legumes and sugar were stored in secret hideouts. In order to bring these to the market he cancelled the maximum prices ordered by the state. The speculators reacted in a flash: Within a few days the shelves in the shops filled and the markets were full of goods and people shopping. Within two weeks the prices dropped by 80 percent and this despite the mounting inflation. He confiscated 600 t olive oil which a German company had bought and put it on the market in Athens. Transport routes were repaired and locomotives overhauled. Neubacher himself was astonished about what he had achieved. His action had surpassed all of what he had hoped for.[2]

However there was another problem which urgently needed a solution: the exchange rate between RM and Drachmae. The Reichsbank wanted to stick to its fictive course of 1:60 because the galloping inflation would have demanded a constant adaptation which was simply impossible. This exchange rate had nothing to do with reality. It enabled Greek students to live in Germany like princes. Merchants had incredibly high gains. Neubacher reports: *"Ein Grieche kaufte eine Maschine aus Deutschland und zahlte brav auf der Grundlage des mehrhundertfach überholten Kurses für den Gegenwert von 1000 RM 60.000 Drachmen ins Clearing; die Maschine verkaufte er sofort an die deutsche Wehrmacht um 25 Millionen Drachmen, die er natürlich sofort in und Waren verwandelte. Kofferweise wurden Papierdrachmen nach Deutschland geschmuggelt. [...] Auslandsdeutsche in Griechenland überwiesen nach Deutschland Vermögen, die sie nie gehabt hatten. Schiebungen ohne Ende!"*[3] Greek importers made fabulous gains and the exporters had extreme losses. Therefore it is not astonishing that the second account could never be settled.

Even on the cultural sector excessive gains were made: *"Die Kulturabteilung der deutschen Gesandtschaft war besonders stolz auf einen geradezu atemberaubenden Siegeszug des deutschen Buches. Die deutsche Buchhandlung wurde überlaufen, unscheinbare Griechen, die kein Wort deutsch sprachen, kauften Goethe, Kant und Schopenhauer, wuchtige wissenschaftliche Werke - sie nahmen in ihrer Begeisterung für das deutsche Buch einfach alles. Ich hörte diese stolze Schilderung mit tiefem Mißtrauen und ging der Sache nach: die Mehrzahl dieser Verehrer der deutschen Literatur verkaufte die schönen Bücher, die für Deutsche längst nicht mehr zu haben waren, ein paar hundert Schritte weiter nach Gewicht an einen Altpapierhändler. Das Geschäft - eine Reichsmark gleich 60 Drachmen - war glänzend.[...] Ein Grieche, dem eine inkassofähige Differenz entgeht, ist kein Grieche. Und in Griechenland leben lauter Griechen!"*[4]

DEGRIGES und SACIG

It was clear that this could not continue because it would have ruined the German-Greek exchange of goods. The German Economic Ministry developed a new construction which was now put in operation. For this purpose a German-Greek Trade Company (DEGRIGES) was created. The Italians did the same and founded the SACIG (Socitá Anonima Commerciale Italiana). Neubacher explains in his memoirs how these two companies functioned.

"Ich komme auf meinen Maschinen-Händler zurück. Dieser zahlte wie bisher für den in Rechnung gestellten Wert von 1000 Mark seine 60 000 Drachmen in die Verrechnungskasse der Notenbank, aber erhielt die Maschine erst dann aus dem Zollverschluss, wenn er einen

1 *Ibidem*, p. 83.
2 *Ibidem*, p. 79.
3 *Ibidem*, p. 80.
4 *Ibidem*, p. 81.

weiteren von einem Aufschleusungskomitee der jeweiligen Marktlage angepaßten Aufschleusungsbetrag bei der 'Degriges' erlegt hatte, der ihm noch einen erstrebenswerten Nutzen übrigließ. Dieser Händler war ob dieser Neuerung der Dinge sehr traurig, weil ihm nach den herrlichen Geschäften der Vergangenheit ein Gewinn von 20-50 % einfach ruinös erschien - aber er handelte weiter. Diese Aufschleusungsbeträge wurden zu 3/5 für den Ankauf griechischer Waren zu freien Marktpreisen verwendet. Auch in diesem Falle wurden die Ankaufspreise über das Clearing mit 60 Drachmen für die Mark verrechnet, aber die Differenz auf den freien Marktpreis dem griechischen Lieferanten aus der Aufschleusungskasse bezahlt. 2/5 der Aufschleusungserlöse wurden für die Abdeckung der Besatzungskostenkredite verwendet."[1]

The work of DEGRIGES and SACIG was of mutual benefit. Greek goods such as tobacco and raisins could be exported to Germany for prices which were inflation-adjusted. A part of the gains was used to reduce the occupation cost of the second account.

The situation of the Greek finances and supplies had improved in October and November 1942 so much that on 1 December Neubacher and Gotzamanis and PM Logothetopoulos signed an agreement that from 1 April 1943 on, the occupation cost which surpassed the regular legal cost would be paid from the gains made by the sale of the imported goods by DEGRIGES and SAGIC. And it was further agreed that these gains would also be used to pay back in rates the advance payments paid until 31 March 1943. From this date the occupation cost should not surpass the 8 million Drachmae barrier.

Neubacher hoped that by then the works for the defence of Greece would be finished and the note printer could be stopped. At the same time Logothetopoulos stated that he would resign if the occupiers would demand higher amounts after the 31 March 1943. With satisfaction he noticed that during his time in office the exchange rate of the sovereign had been stable between 130.000 und 150.000 Drachmae.

At the same time he demanded that the military authorities economized. From now on construction projects over 5,000 RM needed a permit by the Wehrmachtsbefehlshaber Südost. In order to hinder a competition of the three parts of the Wehrmacht when buying material they buying was concentrated in the hands of the officer responsible for economics. In order to prohibit a fresh push to the food prices the buying was confined to vegetables and fruits.[2]

But Rommel's retreat in North Africa triggered new orders to build defence installations which all came to Neubacher. He stalled as much as he could but many of them he had to pass on to the Greek government in the form of new demands of credits. The results were increasing inflation and mounting prices.[3] In order to reduce the cost for the work force it was tried to mobilize civilians but this led to strikes of the worker EAM (EEAM) and prohibited the realization of the program.[4]

Neubacher's Action

By the construction of military buildings the inflation began to move again. The upward movements of the prices could not efficiently be slowed down by the DEGRIGES money. The rate for shot upwards and in November 1943 the horrifying level of 2 million Drachmae. Since the Italians were out of the game by their change of side and Altenburg had been relocated Neubacher and the consul general Graevenitz had to try to get the situation under

1 *Ibidem*, p. 82.
2 Politisches Archiv des Auswärtigen Amts R 27320, p. 84.
3 Neubacher, *op. cit.*, p. 86.
4 Woodhouse, *op. cit.*, p. 135.

control. In August Neubacher had been promoted to "Sonderbevollmächtigten des Auswärtigen Amtes für den Südosten" (Special Agent of the AA for the Southeast). When the situation became constantly worse he developed another unorthodox idea.

In early November Neubacher flew to Berlin where he conferred with the minister of economic affairs, Funk, finance minister, v. Schwerin-Krosigk, the vice-president of the Reichsbank and several other governmental representatives. They agreed that Neubacher should receive 1 million sovereigns (24 million RM) in 6 monthly rates of 6 million RM each to defend the Greek currency. The monthly rate would cover the occupation cost of the Wehrmacht.[1] Already on his flight back to Athens Neubacher carried quite portion of with him.

A few days after his return Neubacher started his first action at the Athens stock exchange. In his memoirs he described it: *"Die Überraschung der Griechen war ungeheuer. Kein Mensch hätte es für möglich gehalten, dass Deutschland Gold auf den Markt wirft. Der Verkauf von 20.000 Pfunden an einem Börsenvormittag genügte, um den Kurs des Pfundes von 2 Millionen auf 900.0000 zu drücken. Sofort war eine Baisse-Partei zur Stelle, die gleichfalls anbot. [...] Der Sinn der Aktion war folgender: die aufgekauften Banknotenmengen wurden für die Deckung der Besatzungskosten verwendet, dadurch wurde die Banknotenpresse entlastet. [...] So blieb die Papierdrachme, die wirklich nur reines Papier war, trotz einer uferlosen Inflation Geld. Die Löhne wurden auf Grund eines Lebenskostenindex laufend den Preisen angepaßt."*[2]

Neubacher accomplished it by his regular gold sales that the Drachmae retained its character as money until the withdrawal of the Wehrmacht from Greece. The returns of the action were used to cover the occupation cost of the second account. The occupation cost fluctuating between 16 and 75 percent were covered.[3]In May 1944 Berlin reduced the number of en coins which were sent monthly to Neubacher causing a revival of the inflation.[4]

However it may stated that the president of the Reichsbank Paul Hahn was right, *"dass ohne die einschneidenden Manipulationen der aktion die 'Vergasung' der griechischen Währung schon zu einem früheren [...] eingetreten wäre. Wenn im September und Oktober 1944 das Inflationstempo gewaltig beschleunigt und schließlich die Trillionengrenze überschritten wurde, so war dieser Tatbestand neben der ungünstig zu beurteilenden Kriegslage auf dem Balkan auch dem nur in geringem Umfange noch verfügbaren bestand zuzuschreiben."*[5]

Afer the German retreat he inflation reached astronomical proportions. In October 1944 1 sovereign cost 1,3 billion Drachmae. The whole existing Greek money could have been bought for 100,000 pounds. The final report of the Reichsbank of April 1945 mirror the currency fall as the following table shows clearly.

Occupation cost from August 1941 to October 1944[6]

1941	9,5 billion Drachmae
1942	137, 9 billion Drachmae
1943	1.351,9 billion Drachmae
1944	465.947,4 billion Drachmae

1 Politisches Archiv des Auswärtigen Amts R 27320, p. 35. On page 57 is the list of the monthly per cental parts.
2 Neubacher, *op. cit.*, p. 87f.
3 Politisches Archiv des Auswärtigen Amts R 27320, p. 38.
4 Politisches Archiv des Auswärtigen Amts R 27320, p. 38.
5 Politisches Archiv des Auswärtigen Amts R 27320, p.41.
6 *Ibidem*, p. 97.

After the withdrawal of the German troops the inflation reached such a dimension that the Drachmae lost its character as money. The British currency specialist David Waley ordered a currency devaluation. 29 billion old Drachmae became one new Drachmae. This improved the situation considerably but it took quite some time until the inflation really ended.[1]

Logothetopoulos and the Occupation Loan

Logothetopoulos' memoirs contain a long passage about the so-called occupation loan which bears the title "Geldabhebungen für Auslagen und Vorauszahlungen" (withdrawing money for expenses and advance payments).[2] In it one reads that the court of the trial against the collaborators found out that the Italians and Germans had withdrawn altogether the equivalent value of 9.097.000 sovereigns. The statements of the general director of the finance ministry Athanasios Sbarounis and of the intendant of the army brigade general Skarvelis made it clear that the "legal" which corresponded with the Hague Convention were 4.100.000 sovereigns. The "illegal" part amounted to 4.996.000 [4.997.000] sovereigns. The governments of Tsolakoglou paid 1.753.000, Logothetopoulos 1.753.000, and Rallis 2.613.000 sovereigns, i.e. alltogether 4.996.000 sovereigns.[3]

Logothetopoulos wrote further: *"Ein Großteil dieser Auslagen wurde für die gleichzeitigen griechischen Bedürfnisse ausgegeben, wie für Straßenbau, für die Ausbesserung und den Bau von Kasernen, Gebäuden usw., die letzten Endes dem Griechischen Staate zugute kamen. Für die vierjährige Besatzungszeit stellte sich dieser Betrag, nach unserer Berechnung, auf 1.000.000 engl. pfund . [...] Wenn wir zu diesem Betrag noch die unbezahlten 1.500 000 engl. pfund [...] für stattgefundene Importe aus Deutschland hinzurechnen, [...] und dazu noch die ca. 1.500.000 engl. pfund, welche die Deutschen während der Regierung I. Rallis eingeführt und durch die Bank von Griechenland auf den Geldmarkt warfen, wie von kompetenter Seite vor Gericht ausgesagt wurde, und zusätzlich noch engl. pfund 1.000.000, die sie einführten und durch die Deutsche Gesellschaft für Zementschiffbau für ihre dringendsten Bedürfnisse auf den Markt warfen, im ganzen also engl. pfund 5.000.000, die eingeführt oder im Lande verbraucht wurden, und durch welche ungeachtet jeder unserer anderen oben erwähnten wohlbegründeten Behauptung, der Betrag, der von dem willkürlichen Urteil des Gerichts den Regierungen als von den Fremden 4.947.000 engl. pfund zu unrecht erhoben angerechneten, auf jeden Fall gedeckt wird."*

If we add the German numbers we arrive at the sum of 5,000,000 sovereigns. Thus Greece owed 3,000 or 4,000 sovereigns to Germany since the retreat of the German troops. If there exists the impression that Germany left debts of 476 million RM in Greece when the Wehrmacht withdrew the explanation is rather simple: Only page 114 of the report of the Reichsbank of 12 April 1945 was taken notice of where a residual debt of that magnitude is mentioned.[4] The statement, which I already mentioned, on page 156 contains the Greek debts to Germany and it simply was not taken notice of. There one reads: *"Man hat den Achsenmächten den Vorwurf gemacht, Griechenland über Gebühr für Kriegsleistungen in Anspruch genommen zu haben. [...] Die aufgeblähten Zahlen der griechischen Leistungen dürfen aber nicht über die großen, keineswegs billigen Anstrengungen der um ihre Existenz ringenden Achsenmächte für die Unterstützung Griechenlands hinwegtäuschen. Es wäre wertvoll, den*

1 Heinz A. Richter, *Geschichte Griechenlands im 20. Jahrhundert, II, 1939-2004* (Ruhpolding: Rutzen, 2015), pp. 194, 210.

2 Richter, *Logothetopoulos*, pp. 148-152.

3 The sum which Logothetopoulos mentions is 4.996.000 sovereigns. The sum of 4.997.000 sovereign is rounded.

4 Politisches Archiv des Auswärtigen Amts R 27320, p. 114.

Beitrag Griechenlands zur Kriegsführung der Achsenmächte und die materielle Hilfe, die die Achsenmächte Griechenland während der Dauer der Besetzung zuteil werden liessen, bilanzmäßig gegenüberzustellen. Bedauerlicherweise muss es diesen Ausführungen versagt bleiben, die deutschen Passive zahlenmässig durch die entsprechenden Aktive zu ergänzen, weil hierfür die Unterlagen noch ausstehen. Auch ohne einen ins einzelne gehenden Nachweis steht ausser Zweifel, dass das Reich durch Lebensmittellieferungen aus seinem eigenen Versorgungsraum, durch den Export von deutschen Waren, die z.T. im Reich Mangelgüter waren, und durch Zurverfügungstellung von aus den beschränkten Eigenbeständen sein Möglichstes getan hat, die Lage in Griechenland zu erleichtern."[1]

As we have shown this report contains concrete references on German compensation payments. It is astonishing that this passage and other references on German compensation payments have not been mentioned in historical studies. And it is even more astonishing that the concrete reference of the Greek passive balance of accounts on page 33 was omitted which reads: *"Bei Abschluss des deutsch-griechischen Verrechnungsverkehrs nach Räumung Griechenlands dürfte der griechische Passivsaldo [...] den Betrag von 300 Mio RM erreicht haben."*[2] This sum corresponds with the 4,000 sovereigns.

Legends

In Greece one often hears the opinion that Neubacher's one million en coins were the "Jewish " confiscated from the Jews by Wisliceny. This can be countered with the evidence that already in October 1942 the Jewish community was not able to pay the 3,5 billion Drachmae (approximately 15,000 sovereigns) for the payoff of the Jewish forced labourers. The missing sum was obtaimed by the sale of the Jewish cemetery to the town of Salonika. The Jewish community of Thessaloniki was by far not as rich as is often heard.

The so-called "Jewish " were rings, bracelets and other en jewelry. This and the whole Jewish liquid funds of the Jews of Salonika had to handed over to the SS. The total value was allegedly 280 billion Drachmae. However in view of the galloping inflation the real value was scarcely higher than the payoff sum. The idea that the Jews of Thessaloniki handed one million over to the SS is absurd. Besides that two thirds of Neubacher's en coins were French en Francs and one third sovereigns. How French francs found their way to the Jews of Salonika nobody could explain this to me.

Another even more absurd legend is that Neubacher's coins were melted Jewish jewelry. Nobody could explain to me how a million en francs and sovereigns could be made in Berlin. The one million en coins stemmed from the Reichsbank. However this does not fit with the Greek imagination of the world,.nor does the fact that the Germans delivered food after all they had been guilty of the famine of 1941. And by the delivery of the goods German companies made immense gains.

But let us return to the compulsory loan. Since the present financial crisis began Athens newspapers wrote that at the end of 1942 a compulsory loan had been imposed on Greece. The amount grew on the basis of low interest to 11 billion Euros. The German historian Götz Aly wrote: *"Die Umrechnung erscheint mir plausibel, doch bezweifle ich die genannte Schuld. Anders Hagen Fleischer, ein deutsch-griechischer Historiker, der die Legende von der 'Zwangsanleihe' seit Jahren hegt und pflegt. Fleischer stützt sich nur auf eine Quelle, nämlich den 251 Blatt starken Schlussbericht, den deutsche Finanz- und*

1 *Ibidem*, p. 156.
2 *Ibidem*, p. 33.

Wirtschaftsbeamte am 12. April 1945 fertigstellten. [...] Wer den Bericht im Politischen Archiv des Auswärtigen Amtes (Signatur R27320) genau liest, stellt fest: Hagen Fleischer zitiert das Dokument in einseitiger Weise; er pickt sich die Aktiva zugunsten Griechenlands heraus und verschweigt die Passiva. Ich kritisiere die verfälschende Interpretation eines einzelnen Dokuments."[1]

I met Hagen Fleischer several years ago in Athens, when my book on the Operation *Mercury* was presented, I told him that I intended to study the problem of the loan. He informed me about the 1945 report of the Reichsbank and sent me a photocopy of it. When I wrote my book on Elisabeth and Konstantinos Logothetopoulos I read the report of the Reichsbank and made the same discovery as Götz Aly. Aly's article was then unknown to me. Fleischer had left aside the page 156. I did not want to attack him personally and therefore I wrote about studies which did not mention this page without mentioning Fleischer's name.

In the meantime in the context of my trial in Crete Fleischer attacked me massively and insinuated that I would manipulate sources. As a historian I am obliged to include all historically and politically critical sources and if they tell the truth include them in my writing. Hagen Fleischer made in the case of the report of the Reichsbank exactly that which he blames me. He falsified history. Despite the criticism in German papers and journals he continues to do this as is shown in his interview in *Griechenland Zeitung*. a few weeks ago, in which he again mentioned the 476 billions RM debt advising Germany to repay at least 10 billion Euros for it.[2]

1 Götz Aly, "Griechische Schuldenlegenden" *Berliner Zeitung* (24. Februar 2015), p. 4.

2 Celine Rebling "Vermittler der griechischen Sicht auf schmerzhafte Besatzungszeit" *Griechenland Zeitung* (3. Oktober 2018), p. 10 and interview: „Über die schwere Zeit der deutschen Okkupation".

CONCLUSIONS

The population of each European state has its myths and legends even tales which is not disquieting as long as it is a kind of popular belief. The same applies for Greece. Such elements often play a part in defining identity or help to overcome weaknesses and mistakes of the past and are therefore necessary. The six-weeks myth strengthens the Greek self assurance. All this is innocuous and harmless as long as it circulates in the population and not in the politics of a country.

Such myths and legends become precarious if they find their way into the internal policy of a country and influence it. The myth of the communist revolution in December 1944 influenced Greece's internal policy during the time of the cold war and had great influence in the internal political dispute. Moreover it prohibited a critical glance at the former protective power Great Britain.

However these views become critical if they influence the foreign policy of a country. The one-sided assignment of guilt in the context of the famine in winter 1941 and the contention that Merten had been the greatest war criminal who was up to mischief in Greece during the occupation led to the tension to project assignment of guilt abroad. If the historical truth is replaced by legends and as in the case of the reparations and the occupation loan become parts of the actual foreign policy or concrete demands it becomes dangerous.

It poisons the internal political climate of Europe. If it is insinuated that Germany is acting as a fourth Reich it is destroying the substance of the European Union. The EU was created out of two motives: Never again war and reconciliation by clearing the horrible past. In Germany this rehabilitation was done thoroughly and in most of Western Europe though not with the same thoroughness. The projection of demonstrably untrue myths and legends n the final analysis undermine the European Union.

If certain German political circles consider the Greek myths and legends as the historical truth then the internal political climate of Germany is also poisoned. It is high time that our thoughts return to the beginning of the European unification process and that we do not concede myths and legends any influence on the actual policy.

INDEX OF NAMES